Praise
The Author's
Building an Onl

❝I like to think I'm pretty savvy when it comes to promoting my books, but Stephanie Chandler's guide taught me new things about navigating Amazon.com's many (confusing) marketing options for authors, generating unique ideas for selling my books, and locating helpful resources. *The Author's Guide to Building an Online Platform* **will help you too, from building your first website to selling your books through affiliates to landing profitable speaking gigs. Promoting books is hard work that every author needs to do, but Chandler's guide makes it easy—and even fun!❞**

—Linda Formichelli, coauthor of *The Renegade Writer,* Lindaformichelli.com

❝The wise author knows that an online presence is essential. Chandler's savvy book is sure to help you sell more books!❞

—John Kremer, consultant and author of *1001 Ways to Market Your Books,* BookMarket.com

❝Due to the Internet, book promoting is now faster, easier, less expensive, and more fun. Stephanie Chandler is on the leading edge of this new way to get your book noticed. Her breakthrough book will guide you through modern book promotion.❞

—Dan Poynter, author of *The Self-Publishing Manual,* ParaPublishing.com

❝Ms. Chandler gives you all the tips you will need to flourish as an author, plus countless more that you didn't even know you needed. Each page is rich with nuggets that illuminate the path for writers.❞

—Jay Conrad Lavinson, author of *Guerrilla Marketing,* Guerrillamarketingassociation.com

❝As someone who has worked with authors and speakers for an entire lifetime, this book is a welcome addition to the industry. It is nearly impossible to build a career as an expert on any subject without an online presence. Chandler's book is well-written and is filled with sound advice and strategies that can benefit any author, new or experienced.❞

—Lilly Walters, author of *Speak and Grow Rich,* Lillywalters.com

"Here's a primer telling you where to focus, who to see, and what to do online with your own book. Partner this publication with your own, and you'll measure your sales in thousands instead of dozens."

—C. Hope Clark, editor, FundsforWriters.com

"It is about time that someone wrote this book, and it is sure to become a staple for authors at every level. Building recognition online is one of the most important ways to achieve success, and Chandler's book provides the guidelines you've been waiting for. If you want to accelerate your success as an author, buy this book now!"

—Dr. Joe Vitale, author of *The Attractor Factor* and *The Key*, Mrfire.com

"Authors today must wear many hats besides just 'Author.' While that's not always welcome news, books like Stephanie Chandler's give a much needed reality check about the publishing world today, and how to win big at the online publicity game—crucial to any author seeking commercial success. Highly recommended."

—Peter Bowerman, author of *The Well-Fed Writer* series, Wellfedwriter.com

"Whether you've already successfully built a platform or are working to establish yourself as an expert in a new area, you'll learn great new tricks to boost your expert status and enhance your credibility. From promoting your blog to approaching bloggers to write about your book, marketing with video, starting an online group, or using online social networking sites to connect with readers, this book has it all. Chock-full of great tips, leads, and ideas you can start to use immediately. Buy this book!"

—Marcia Layton Turner, award-winning author, Becomeasixfigurewriter.com

"As an author for numerous Chicken Soup for the Soul titles and other books, I know the importance of marketing. Stephanie Chandler's book offers tremendous value in a highly competitive industry. If you want to be successful as an author, there are many priceless lessons here. You may only regret that you didn't find this book sooner!"

—Dahlynn McKowen, coauthor of *Chicken Soup for the Soul* series,
    PublishingSyndicate.com

The Author's Guide to Building an Online Platform

Leveraging the Internet to Sell More Books

Stephanie Chandler

Sanger, California

Printed in the United States of America.

Published by
Quill Driver Books/Word Dancer Press, Inc.,
1254 Commerce Way, Sanger, CA 93657
559-876-2170 / 800-497-4909
QuillDriverBooks.com

Quill Driver Books' titles may be purchased for educational, fund-raising, business or promotional use. Please contact Special Markets, Quill Driver Books/Word Dancer Press, Inc. at the above address or phone numbers.

Quill Driver Books/Word Dancer Press Project Cadre:
Doris Hall, Linda Kay Hardie, Christine Hernandez, Stephen Blake Mettee

First Printing

ISBN 1-884956-82-3 • 978-1884956-82-9

**To order a copy of this book, please call
1-800-497-4909.**

To my son, Benjamin, who lights up my world in the most
wonderful ways.

Library of Congress Cataloging-in-Publication Data
Chandler, Stephanie, 1972-
The author's guide to building an online platform : leveraging the
Internet to sell more books / by Stephanie Chandler.
p. cm.
Includes index.
ISBN 978-1-884956-82-9
1. Authorship—Marketing. 2. Books—Marketing. 3. Electronic com-
merce. I. Title.
PN161.C43 2008
070.5068'8—dc22

2008001504

Contents

Acknowledgments

I would like to thank the authors who provided interviews for this book: Scott Allen, Karen Gillespie, Diana Ennen, Dan S. Kennedy, Hal Elrod, Michelle Dunn, Jill Lublin, and Barbara Winter. Each contribution offers tremendous value to readers. I love real-world insight and plan to continue interviewing experts for all of the books that I write.

This book was sort of an accident. In 2007, I scheduled lunch with Andrea Hurst, a literary agent I met at the San Francisco Writer's Conference several years earlier (note to aspiring writers: writer's conferences are an excellent investment in your dreams!). We kept in touch and finally set a meeting to discuss my new book ideas. I brought her a copy of a workbook that I was selling through my website called *Online Marketing for Authors* because I thought it might be useful to some of her clients.

While I rattled off a list of ideas about business books, Andrea thumbed through the workbook and then interrupted my rant with, "I think I can sell this." This possibility hadn't even occurred to me. I've been creating information products and e-books to sell through my site for years and this was another quiet little revenue-generator for me. I was immediately excited at the chance to expand my audience and reach some of my favorite people: writers.

Thank you, Andrea, for keeping in touch over the years and making this book possible. Thank you, also, to Steve Mettee at Quill

Driver Books for providing valuable insight and for having confidence in my abilities.

I couldn't write this section without acknowledging my family. My dad frequently jokes that I should publicly thank him at all of my speaking engagements. He threatens to show up at events so he can get recognition for his role in my life, and I suppose he deserves some. For you Dad: "Thank you to my father. Without his brilliance and amazing wisdom, I would not be where I am today!" Are you happy now?

Thanks also to my mom, AKA Grandma, who steps in to cover for me anytime I need help at home. At this writing, my son Ben is an active toddler (that's putting it lightly—he's more like a wild dog on a sugar high with his tail on fire). Ben keeps us all on our toes and grandma is always eager to spend time with him. Because it doesn't feel like work to her, she has no idea just how much she helps me on a regular basis and how much I appreciate her.

My husband, Chris, gets the biggest thanks of all. When I announced in 2002 that I wanted to quit my high-paying Silicon Valley job to pursue my dreams, Chris barely flinched. He told me to go for it and has continued to support all of my aspirations, no matter how crazy they may have seemed. I'm fairly certain that there aren't too many people out there who would have that kind of faith—myself included—and that is a spectacular gift.

Introduction

In 2003 I made the most important decision of my life—I kissed off corporate America and left skid marks on my way out. I had spent 11 years in the Silicon Valley and rode the wave of the Dot Com Boom and survived the Dot Com Bust. I watched businesses close, friends lose jobs, and the traffic on the Bay Area freeways decline as a result of the local economy.

Through the economic turmoil, I was working in software sales and carrying a $4 million quota. Though the financial rewards were plentiful, I dreaded my 12-hour workdays. Eventually the pressure took a toll on my health. After carrying a bottle of Maalox around in briefcase for months and ultimately fainting at a sales conference in Las Vegas, I was diagnosed with an ulcer. It was clearly time for a major lifestyle change.

When I searched my soul for an answer to the age old question, *What do I want to be when I grow up?*, I kept coming back to my childhood dream: I wanted to be a writer. But since I didn't yet know how to earn a living as a writer, I chose the next best option. I moved to Sacramento and opened a bookstore.

My plan was to get the store up and running, put a staff in place, and build a passive-income business that would allow me time to write novels and articles for women's magazines. But in the process of quitting my job and opening the store, many people said to me, "I wish I had the courage to do what you did." I saw pain in the eyes of my friends who felt trapped in corporate

America. With families at home and endless responsibility, many thought it impossible to leave it all behind to pursue a dream.

But for me, it didn't feel like a courageous act. I had carefully planned my departure for more than a year. I read countless books, spent hours conducting research on the Internet, wrote a 42-page business plan, saved money like a bear storing up for a long winter, and felt elated on my last day as an employee.

The Fork in the Road

"If there is a book you really want to read but it hasn't been written yet, then you must write it."
—Toni Morrison

It occurred to me that I had acquired a tremendous amount of information and experience in the process of starting my business. And though I had read dozens of business start-up guides, none had answered all of my questions. I decided that I would take Toni Morrison's advice and write the book that I wanted to read!

I got to work immediately, outlining the book, chiseling away at the chapters. I devoted several hours per day to the project while simultaneously running my new bookstore and building a freelance writing portfolio with various magazines and newspapers.

I also read several books about getting published and began querying editors and agents. To my surprise, many wrote back and some even asked to see a proposal and sample chapters. But the same question appeared with each response: "What's your platform?"

After attending a writer's conference, one well-known agent took the time to call me and asked the dreaded platform question. He told me that I should be speaking to tens of thousands of people across the country so that I would have a ready-made audience of book buyers because that's what publishers want.

When I pointed out that his suggestion was like putting the cart before the horse and that once I had a published book, I would be more likely to be invited to speak to people, he said he couldn't argue the point but it was a dilemma that I needed to solve. He couldn't help me until I had a viable platform.

Time was of the essence. Patience has never been one of my virtues and I was eager to move forward with my publishing goals.

When I thought about ways to quickly build a platform (preferably without leaving the comfort of my home), it occurred to me that the Internet provided tremendous opportunities.

I conducted some research on business-related websites and discovered some weaknesses there. Most just covered the basics: how to write a business plan, how to market a business, etc. There was a need for a website that offered more. For example, none of the sites provided industry-specific resources for starting various kinds of businesses.

Before I could talk myself out of it, I launched BusinessInfoGuide.com, a directory of resources for entrepreneurs. It includes resource guides for starting all kinds of businesses including restaurants, pet services, retail stores, and much more. I began filling the site with articles and links to useful information. I started promoting a monthly e-zine and sent the first edition out to a grand total of eight subscribers.

The Turning Point

As I learned new strategies for marketing BusinessInfoGuide.com, as well as for marketing myself as a small business expert, the site traffic began to grow—quickly. I moved forward with my first book, *The Business Startup Checklist and Planning Guide: Seize Your Entrepreneurial Dreams!* I couldn't stand to wait to find a publisher, so I hired the best resources I could find (an editor, a cover designer, and a great print-on-demand publisher) and released the book in September 2005.

I began promoting the book release on my website and to my great surprise and delight; I started receiving orders a full two months before the book was released. That was the moment when I understood what the publishers meant by having a platform.

It turns out that most of us buy books based on recommendations. Whether from friends, book reviews in print publications, or through books promoted in various online venues. A recommendation from another source carries a tremendous amount of weight. But a lot can also be said for being a recognized expert in your field and building an eager audience of readers.

Finally, a Publisher!

As I continued to build BusinessInfoGuide.com, I decided that I wanted to sell e-books and special reports. After all, I had an audience eager for business-related information and I had no short-age of topics I wanted to write about. As I always do when I want to learn something new, I looked for a book that would teach me how to make money from information products but to my sur-prise, no such book existed.

After studying how various Internet marketers were compil-ing, promoting, and selling their information products, I launched my first products. They began selling immediately.

Can you guess what happened next?

I wrote a proposal for a new book called *From Entrepreneur to Infopreneur: Make Money with Books, e-books and Information Products*. I sent the proposal and two sample chapters, along with a market-ing plan and description of my high-traffic website, to two publish-ers. John Wiley and Sons made me an offer a month later.

Why? Because I had a viable platform. With thousands of visi-tors to BusinessInfoGuide.com each month, an active speaking schedule, thousands of subscribers to my monthly e-zine, and plenty of media recognition, I had built an expert platform and credibility that captured the interest of a reputable publisher.

The Evolution of this Book

I went to have lunch with a literary agent, Andrea Hurst, who was interested in working with me to further advance my business book writing career. As we discussed my current book ideas, I handed her a copy of a workbook I had written called *Online Marketing for Authors*. It was a product I sold through BusinessInfoGuide.com and I thought some of her author clients might find it useful.

She thumbed through the guide while I rambled on about my ideas and then she announced, "I think I can sell this." It hadn't even occurred to me to pursue a book deal since I was so focused on writing business material. It also never occurred to me that one of my information products could find a home with a publisher.

The good folks at Quill Driver Books, more specifically Steve Mettee, agreed that the book had a place in the market. We changed the title and expanded the focus, and I began contacting authors, asking them to contribute their knowledge and experience in the form of interviews. The results are peppered throughout this book, and provide a tremendous amount of real-world advice.

I understand the challenges that are involved in book marketing. I decided to write this book because I have seen too many authors who either aren't marketing their books at all or who are missing major opportunities to promote their books online.

It seems that many authors believe that conducting book signing events is somehow the ultimate in book marketing. I hate to break the news to you, but this is probably one of the *least effective* ways to market a book. Sure you can get some public attention through the foot traffic that passes by your table or even a mention in the local newspaper—and these benefits aren't without merit. But the average number of books sold at a signing event is somewhere around eight copies. Yikes!

In a survey called "The Business Impact of Writing a Book" issued by RainToday.com, the authors surveyed indicated their top marketing tactics (listed here in order of popularity):

1. Internet marketing
2. Trade magazine coverage
3. Marketed to existing clients
4. Newspaper coverage
5. Marketed by association
6. Marketed to own newsletter list
7. Third-party newsletter coverage
8. Directly to companies
9. Radio coverage
10. Marketed through catalogs
11. Marketed directly to bookstores
12. Marketed to colleges/graduate schools
13. Trade show marketing
14. TV coverage
15. Book signing events
16. Marketed to libraries

One of the many advantages of internet marketing is the opportunity to reach potential readers around the globe. In most cases it doesn't require a big cash investment to spread the word about your book—your biggest investment will be in your time. But with the right amount of effort, you should begin to see results rather quickly.

As authors, we all share similar goals: we want people to read and enjoy our books, we don't want our efforts to be in vain, and we want our books to be a success. My intention with this book is to help you make the most of your publishing journey and to realize your dreams. You've done the hardest work—you've transferred words to paper. Now let's go out and sell those words and make a difference in some readers' lives!

CHAPTER 1

The Truth About Publishing

Getting published has some tremendous benefits. First and foremost, it can be incredibly rewarding. There are also some amazing advantages that you may not have considered.

As an author, you:

- ✓ Instantly become an expert in your subject matter.
- ✓ Have the best business card available. A book can open many doors of opportunity.
- ✓ Can find it easier to schedule speaking engagements. In fact, these opportunities will find you if you're marketing correctly.
- ✓ Develop a celebrity status both locally and online.
- ✓ Can use your book to grow your business (if they are related).
- ✓ Will have the opportunity to continue publishing additional books if you can make your first book a success.

As an author and former bookstore owner, I have seen many authors who market their books well and even more authors who don't market their books at all. It's easy to fall back on the belief that you've done the work by writing the book in the first place, but like it or not, that's when the work is just beginning.

The reality in the world of publishing is that without marketing, a book simply cannot be successful. And even if you have the biggest publisher on the planet behind you, it is unlikely that they will run your entire marketing campaign for you. You will still be required to do the majority of the work.

Whether you already have one or several books in print or your first book is a work-in-progress, marketing should be at the top of your mind. Every author needs a plan for finding an audience of buyers and it's best if this starts before the book even makes it to print.

How to Dazzle Publishers and Agents

Agents and publishers have one thing in common: they both need to find good authors. You can be the most talented author or have the freshest idea, but if you want to land a publishing contract, you need to have all of the puzzle pieces in place.

Puzzle Piece #1: Get a Fresh Concept

If you take a walk through your favorite bookstore, you will note that in each section, there are a variety of books with similar concepts. There are thousands of cookbooks, marketing books, children's books, fiction novels, self-help guides, astrology books, diet books, business books, reference books and memoirs introduced each year. Your concept doesn't necessarily have to be new, but in order to stand out, it has to be different, timely or relevant in some way.

Michele Scott spent more than ten years attending writer's conferences and looking for a publisher for one of her eight book manuscripts. Finally in 2004, Scott received a three-book contract from Berkley Prime Crime for her Wine Lover's Mystery series.

In the crowded field of mystery books, Scott was able to set her work apart with a unique angle that appealed to a broad audience. Her books include *Murder by the Glass*, *Murder Uncorked* and *Silenced by Syrah*. She has gone on to write a series of mysteries for horse lovers including *Saddled with Trouble* and *Death Reins In*.

This same concept applies for nonfiction. When writing a book proposal, you are expected to include a competition analysis—a list of books that compete with your book. Odds are that your concept isn't unique, but you must demonstrate for agents and editors how it is different from other books that will share shelf space with your title. Once you find a unique way to present your book, you will be well on your way to getting published.

Puzzle Piece #2: Understand the Publishing Business

By reading this book, you are taking the right steps to understanding the publishing industry. Many writers venture out with only a limited picture of what the industry is all about. When you are armed with knowledge, it can make the difference between having doors opened or having them closed right in front of you.

Literary agent Andrea Hurst recommends attending writer's conferences. I couldn't agree more. This is a great place to learn about the publishing industry while making great industry connections. The best conferences have agents and editors on hand who are eagerly seeking new talent. Also, in my own experience, the majority of conference attendees are pitching fiction and memoirs. If you have a different kind of book, you will stand out in the crowded conference rooms. I once attended a conference with hundreds of people and was the only business book writer there. I stood out like a polar bear in the desert and it was great. For a comprehensive listing of writer's conferences all over the world, visit Writing.Shawguides.com.

Most major cities have local writer's groups where you can get feedback on your work and learn about the publishing industry. There are also dozens of associations for writers with a niche focus such as Sisters in Crime and Romance Writers of America. Visit the resources guide at the end of this book for a list of many regional and specialty associations.

You can also find a tremendous amount of information on the Internet. Following are some of the top resources for publishing:

- ✓ You Can Write is a comprehensive resource for nonfiction publishing: youcanwrite.com
- ✓ Fan Story provides workshops and writing assignments for fiction writers: fanstory.com/index
- ✓ Visit Writers.net for resources for writers, agents and publishers: writers.net

✓ Publishing Trends provides news and trends on the publishing world: publishingtrends.com

✓ Publishers Marketplace contains a wealth of industry news and resources: publishersmarketplace.com

Puzzle Piece #3: Find an Agent or Publisher

Though some small and mid-sized publishers allow authors to submit book ideas directly, the largest publishing companies require an author be represented by a literary agent. A literary agent is your advocate in finding and obtaining a good book deal. Agents have experience with contracts, connections in the publishing community and the know-how to find a publisher. An agent will typically take a 15 percent commission, a fee that can pay for itself when the result is a great publishing contract.

There are several ways to locate an agent. The Association of Authors' Representatives (aar-online.org) is a trade association with a strict code of ethics and conduct that its members are required to follow. Another good directory of agents can be found at Another Realm: anotherealm.com/prededitors/pubagent.htm.

When looking for an agent, it's imperative that you conduct research about the agent before you make any contact. Each agent has a different focus and preferences and you will waste your time and the agent's time if you inquire about a genre that the agent doesn't cover.

Most agents have submission guidelines listed on their website. Read and follow these requirements if you want to be considered. Most require that you first send a query letter that briefly describes the book. If the query letter piques their interest, you will likely be invited to send a proposal and sample chapters. This is when things really start to get interesting.

Puzzle Piece #4: Stand Out in a Crowded Field

Because their time is in great demand, you have a limited chance to capture the interest of an agent or publisher. The initial query letter is vitally important. If it is not well-written or does not convey how your work is different or better than the competition, you will likely hit a dead-end.

Convey how great your book is, how it is different from the rest, who the audience is for the book and why you are the best person to author the book.

Once your letter is accepted, the proposal is the next critical step in the process. Every proposal should include the following elements:

1. Book Overview: This should be written to entice the reader and should be two to five pages long.

2. Market Analysis: Explain who is going to want to read this book and why. Indicate any statistics that support your claim.

3. Competitive Analysis: List at least five competing books and how your book is different or better.

4. Marketing Plan: Provide detailed plans for how you will market the book. If you have a high-traffic website, list it here. If you have a large mailing list or conduct a lot of speaking engagements, exploit the details. Agent Andrea Hurst reports that one of her biggest pet peeves is when authors indicate that they will launch a website after the book comes out. Marketing should begin before the book even goes to press.

5. Author Biography: This is not your life history, but should offer a detailed account of your experience *as it relates to the book*. Have you had special training in writing? Are you a known expert in your field? Have you won any awards or received any media coverage? List every impressive detail you can here.

6. Chapter Outline: A detailed list of chapters along with a summary of each chapter is needed here.

7. Sample Chapters: Most agents require two or three sample chapters. Make sure these are your best work. Most important, the first few pages of your first chapter should be extremely engaging.

Andrea Hurst points out that a great book title can make a big difference. "I often get interested in a book initially because it has a great title," says Hurst. Conversely, she is quickly turned off when a title lacks luster.

The overall message here is that you should take time to prepare before you even begin to contact agents or editors. Without a solid book concept, query letter, and proposal, you will simply be treading water.

Puzzle Piece #5: Develop an Undeniable Platform

The formation of a platform is essential for publishing nonfiction and helpful for writers of fiction. A platform encompasses your ability to reach a broad audience before the book is even released.

Because the publishing marketplace has grown more competitive over the years, publishers want authors to come with a built-in audience. If you can demonstrate that you have thousands of people interested in your book through a busy public speaking schedule, a high-traffic website or blog, a substantial newsletter subscriber list or some kind of celebrity status, you are practically guaranteed to find a publisher that wants to work with you.

Of course there are exceptions to every rule. Authors of fiction and gift books aren't always required to have a platform first. But if you come to the table with one, your chances of getting published will be dramatically increased.

Agents and publishers want authors who can sell books. Once you realize this and figure out how to demonstrate that you can do that, your future in publishing will be bright.

This entire book is devoted to helping you develop a platform utilizing online resources for establishing your expertise and seizing online opportunities that will help you sell more books.

Author Interview

Author: Scott Allen

Book: *The Virtual Handshake: Opening Doors and Closing Deals Online* (AMACOM)

Website: TheVirtualHandshake.com

What is your book about?

The Virtual Handshake is the first book to look at how mainstream businesspeople are using social networking, social media and other Web 2.0 technologies to build virtual relationships that lead to real business.

What led you to publish the book?

I was passionate about the topic and had made the decision that it was what I wanted to build my personal brand around. I also felt like there was a good opportunity in the marketplace, both for the book and for consulting and speaking on the topic, and the book would position me as an expert on the topic.

How has being an author changed or improved your life personally or professionally?

Even with the popularity of self-publishing and so many more books being published all the time, there is still a certain mystique around authors among the general population. And it has absolutely opened doors for speaking engagements and consulting opportunities that I wouldn't have had without it.

What online marketing methods have worked best for you?

We started a blog for our book while we were in the process of writing it and built an audience before it even came out.

Overall, that's been by far the best method. Another one that is working well for us now is that we found a sponsor, Landslide, who will give a free copy of our book to people for watching a demo of their product. A $15 book for 20 minutes of your time? A lot of people will do that.

Are there any methods you have used that haven't yielded impressive results?

Actually, all the traditional media coverage has never really done that much for us, at least not directly. It's one thing if you get a feature article written about you, but just being quoted as a source, even in major publications, never caused a noticeable spike in sales or traffic to our website. On the other hand, being able to say, "Quoted in the *Washington Post, Fast Company,* ABCNews.com, CNN.com, *CFO Magazine,* etc.," adds a lot of credibility. Hard to tie that directly to book sales, though. Maybe, but there's no way to track it.

Do you have a favorite off-line book marketing strategy?

Off-line? People market their books off-line?
Seriously though—the most effective off-line strategy I've used is to be at conferences and giving signed copies of my book to thought leaders—preferably bloggers—in related fields. They'll almost always write a review, even if it's brief. Also, I make a point to connect with prominent bloggers when they come into town— we usually try to have some kind of small get-together of business bloggers and invite the out-of town bloggers, and I always give them a signed copy of my book.

Do you own a business?

I do it all—writer, editor, blogger, speaker, consultant. Besides my book, people might best know me as the Entrepreneurs Guide for About.com, but I have dozens of other clients, plus a couple of blogs of my own. I also consult with companies on how to make best use of social media and social networking.

Has being an author helped your business in any way?

Absolutely. We had the first book, and still the preeminent book, on the topic. I don't really go out and directly seek out business much any more—it comes to me.

If you were just getting started in publishing today, is there anything that you would do differently?

While I joked about it above, actually, I'd definitely spend more time on proactive off-line marketing of the book—book signings, speaking engagements, etc. I think we thought more of it was going to just come our way than it did. The other big thing is *make sure your publisher is handling Amazon correctly.* The contents of your book should be searchable. You should be verified as an author so that you can blog on Amazon. The publication date needs to be correct. All three of those were problems for us.

What advice do you have for other authors?

Do it all, and then keep doing what works. I'm convinced now that every single book has its own unique audience and unique appeal, and therefore a different combination of marketing techniques is going to work best for every book. Anyone who says they have the one magic formula for selling a bunch of books every time for every book is lying. Deepak Chopra advertised on TV during Oprah and became a best-seller; Richard Paul Evans did it and didn't even get a slight bump in sales (as told to me by Richard himself). Try anything that's within your budget to try on a small scale, and then do more of whatever gives you results.

Make sure to budget not only money, but your time, to market the book when it comes out. Take a month off from everything else to focus 100 percent on book marketing, or at least as close to that as you possibly can. If you're not prepared to do that, don't be surprised when your book doesn't sell as well as you hoped.

Most important—*network.* Network with other authors; network with your readers; network with people who are interested in the topic/theme of your book. Find the online communities and groups where these people are, then join and participate. It's the lowest-cost marketing you can do (that's still effective).

CHAPTER 2

Website Strategies

Every author should have a website. An author site is useful for dealing with the public (your fans!), contacting editors and publishers, and promoting your work. Your site has the potential to reach millions of people around the globe and is limited only by your imagination.

The following are some author websites to give you some ideas of the variety of ways you can build a traditional author site:

✓ kickstartguy.com
✓ LindaFormichelli.com
✓ BarbaraWinter.com
✓ sfwriter.com

Your website can have a single focus (your book) or it can serve multiple purposes. For example, if you are also a freelance writer, you can use your site to promote your writing abilities and share clips with new editors.

It may also make sense to have more than one website. I have my writer website, StephanieChandler.com, which I have used for promoting my freelance work to editors. But I also have a business website where I market my business books: BusinessInfoGuide.com.

Niche Websites Sell Books

A niche website can help you reach your target audience, impress publishers and media, and most importantly, sell more books. While many authors have certainly been able to achieve success through a basic author website, just as many have figured out that building a targeted site can have tremendous advantages.

Loral Langemeier, author of *The Millionaire Maker's Guide to Creating a Cash Machine for Life*, is also the founder of LiveOutLoud.com. Langemeier promotes her books, seminars and coaching services through her Live Out Loud website and has become well-known as an expert wealth advisor.

Like many successful nonfiction authors who also run related businesses, Langemeier's publishing efforts complement her business and boost her credibility as an expert in her field. As a result, she has been featured in *Forbes*, *BusinessWeek*, CNN, and many other media outlets.

Publicity expert Jill Lublin is the author of *Networking Magic* and a coauthor of *Guerrilla Publicity* with Jay Conrad Levinson. Lublin takes a simple approach to marketing her books through her website, JillLublin.com. However, her books and her business work in harmony to help her schedule more speaking engagements and impress clients of her PR firm.

The original authors of the famed *Chicken Soup for the Soul* series of books, Jack Canfield and Mark Victor Hansen, have grown their essay collections into a true empire. The duo began as motivational speakers and wanted to launch a book that included an anthology of essays. They were rejected by a whopping 140 publishers before Health Communications, Inc. picked up the book and released the first edition in 1993.

Today there are millions of Chicken Soup books in print and visitors to ChickenSoup.com will find details about the newest book releases, guidelines for essay submission, and even Chicken Soup branded pet food and greeting cards.

As a result of the stunning success from the series, Jack Canfield and Mark Victor Hansen have achieved tremendous success and fame. Both have gone on to publish their own respective books and products and market them through their websites: JackCanfield.com and MarkVictorHansen.com.

Fiction Rules Online

Fiction authors are also maximizing the power of the Internet. Visit StephenKing.com for biography, news and an active message board for this iconic author of horror books.

Nicholas Grabowsky, author of *The Everborn* and several other toe-curling horror titles, promotes his work through his website DownWarden.com. Grabowsky also publishes an electronic newsletter and has an active presence on My Space: myspace.com/downwarden.

Chick Lit fans can visit JenniferWeiner.com to read the author's blog and tips for writers. Judy Blume, a beloved children's book author, hosts JudyBlume.com. Visitors can sign the author's guest book (which is full of adorable postings from young fans), read Blume's bio and learn how she got the inspiration for each of her books.

Suspense novelist Lisa Unger hosts a website of the same name. Readers can sign up for her mailing list, listen to the author's podcasts or even watch a video. Francis Ray, author of more than thirty romance novels, has a website that lists details for her current tour, a video about a made-for-TV movie, and a link for visitors to join her Yahoo Group.

The Bottom Line

Whether you write math textbooks, cookbooks, memoirs, science books, business guides, children's stories, or virtually anything set between two covers, opportunities abound on the Internet.

I believe that every author should have a Web presence. A traditional website is the most basic place to start, though more and more authors are finding new and innovative ways to promote online.

For example, if you want a reason to write several times per week, you might consider hosting a blog. In its early days, MySpace.com was a social networking site marketed to teens but today this site is a platform for authors, musicians, business owners, and artists. We will discuss both of these options coming up.

Whatever you decide to do, you're about to learn lots of tricks and tips to help you form a plan for your online success. Not every strategy in this book will work for every author, but you can decide for yourself which strategies will work for you. Just remember to have fun with whatever you do because your readers will notice, and it will make the experience even more worthwhile.

Website Content

Before you begin building your website, it is a good idea to consider what kind of content you plan to include. At a minimum your site should include the following information:

- ✓ Author's bio with any special credentials listed
- ✓ Author's contact information
- ✓ Publicist contact information (if applicable)
- ✓ Clips or links to articles you have published*
- ✓ Clips or links to articles published about you
- ✓ Lists of memberships and affiliations
- ✓ A product page where visitors can purchase your book
- ✓ A separate sales page for each book you have written (if you have more than one) that includes compelling sales copy
- ✓ Book reviews
- ✓ Awards or similar recognition
- ✓ Testimonials
- ✓ Archived press releases
- ✓ Schedule of events/author appearances
- ✓ Excerpts from your book(s)
- ✓ A press kit (more on this later in this chapter)

*Note: In the world of publishing a "clip" is a copy of a published article. On a website, these can be represented by a link to the article on the publication's website or the article can be scanned into a PDF document for viewing on any platform of computer. If you scan the article, make sure you get permission from the publication to publish the clip on your website. Some magazines will actually charge you for the right to do this.

Additional Web Content Ideas

You get to create the rules so be creative when building content for your site. A cookbook author might include recipes or cooking tips. A novelist might write fun letters to readers from the main characters. A scientist could leverage facts and figures. A children's book author could include illustrations or short adventures featuring the main characters.

Here are some additional content ideas:

✓ Sample chapters
✓ Industry news, trends, or data
✓ Newsletter archives
✓ Related business services
✓ Speaker's data sheet (includes topics you speak about)
✓ Contests
✓ Links to favorite websites
✓ Links to useful resources
✓ Articles and essays written by you or others

Assemble an Overview

You may want to have an overview of your book available for a number of reasons. You can use this as part of your press kit for the media, for obtaining quotes and testimonials or for other book promotion opportunities. You can put your overview on a hidden page of your website and send the link out as needed or make it available to all website visitors—depending on how much information you are willing to share. Just keep in mind that your overview should be persuasive and should convince a reader that your book is fantastic.

The following is a list of items to include in your overview:

✓ A good description of the book—similar to your book jacket copy
✓ Table of contents

✓ One or two sample chapters
✓ Any relevant testimonials
✓ A brief author's bio

Press Kit

A press kit is the information you make available to the media. In the event that an editor, reporter, or producer wants to feature you in a story, they may leverage the information in your press kit. In the past it was important to have a hard copy of your press kit, but the Internet has made this requirement nearly obsolete. Today you can post press information directly on your website.

When I owned my bookstore, I frequently received elaborate folders filled with press information from authors. If I'd had more time, I would have called each and suggested they save their money. I suspect that few bookstore personnel or media would take time to review an unsolicited press packet without some compelling reason to do so. It's best to add this information to your website and leave it at that. You can always reference, "Additional press information is available on my website."

When adding this information to your site, you should ideally add an exclusive page called "Press" or "Media" to make this process as easy as possible. An added benefit of listing this information on your website is that it will likely be picked up by search engines and could ultimately result in media people finding out about you through a Web search.

Press Kit Components

✓ Author bio
✓ Press release archives
✓ Photos of you and your book(s) (make sure these are high-resolution)
✓ Previous media coverage (articles, links to media sites, news or radio programs, books you have contributed to, etc.)

✓ Testimonials from others including their contact
information (make sure to get their permission first)
✓ One-page sales sheet about your book
✓ Frequently asked questions with answers
✓ Sample interview questions (radio hosts like these)
✓ Articles you have written
✓ Contact information

The above items may be separate pages on your website or combined on just a few pages. How you format your press information is up to you. Just keep in mind that you want to make it easy for the media to locate any needed information about you and your books.

Outline Your Pages

Create an outline of the content you want to create for your website. You can start by listing page titles such as Home, About the Author, Contact, Media, etc. Then for each page, write down the details and topics you plan to include. This will help you prepare for getting your site designed and will give you an outline for writing your Web copy. Here is an overview of basic Web pages:

Home Page

This page is your first chance to make an impression on readers. It should provide a brief overview about you as an author and your book(s). Include pictures of you and your books. Brief testimonials and powerful sales copy should also be used here.

About

This page describes you, your background and experience as a writer. It can include whatever details you are willing to share. Personalize it by including photos. It can be formal or friendly, depending on the overall tone of your website. You may also want to include links to press information, news releases, or other PR materials in this section if you don't have a separate page for media information.

Contact

In addition to an e-mail address, you may also want to list a mailing address and phone number on your website. If you operate from home, you will want to get a post office box. It just makes good sense to avoid publishing your home address.

Products

Whether you make your books available for sale on your website or not, it's a good idea to offer a description of them along with a link to purchase on Amazon or elsewhere. Include a picture of the book cover, reviews and testimonials and sales copy for your book.

Newsletter/E-zine

Start gathering contact information as soon as your site is live and send a newsletter consistently, even if you only have two subscribers. You may choose to archive previous editions of your newsletter so that site visitors can get an idea what it's all about.

List additional pages and content you plan to include in your website. Some ideas include:

✓ Media Relations
✓ Articles
✓ Calendar of Events
✓ Additional Resources
✓ Favorite Resources
✓ Special Offers

Author Interview

Author: Karin Gillespie

Most recent book: *Earthly Pleasures* (published under the pen name Karen Neches)

Total # of books published: Six

Websites: karingillespie.com and karenneches.com

What is your book about?

It's about a greeter in Heaven who is preparing for her first life on Earth. She takes classes that distill all of life's philosophies into five Beatles songs. She also falls in love with one of her clients who makes an appearance in Heaven during a near-death experience. It's an inter-dimensional love story.

What led you to publish the book?

One day I had this thought: *Lovely Bones* meets *Bridget Jones*. I decided a light novel set in Heaven would be a challenge. Boy was I right about that. The novel took me two years to write and underwent dozens of revisions. Both my editor and agent hated it immediately and I almost gave up on it all together.

How has being an author changed or improved your life personally or professionally?

It has improved it immensely. I feel like writing is what I am meant to do. I enjoy every aspect of the process, including the publicity. I'm the kind of person who eagerly looks forward to Mondays. (Although I also write on weekends as well, just not as much.)

What online marketing methods have worked best for you?

I organized a forty-author virtual tour called the Girlfriend Cyber Circuit. I also have a grog (group blog) for Southern authors called "A Good Blog is Hard to Find"; southernauthors.blogspot.com.

Are there any methods you have used that haven't yielded impressive results?

All online things I've done have worked well. I would caution authors against going on list serves and posting messages merely to promote their books. You need to really be part of things before you shoot your mouth about your book. Offline, I think most book signings are a waste of time.

Do you have a favorite off-line book marketing strategy?

Yes. I try very hard to connect with indie booksellers by encouraging them to read my ARCs and make comments.

Do you write full-time?

Yes. It's truly a full-time job, especially when you factor in all the time for publicity efforts. I would probably teach writing if I couldn't make a living at it.

If you were just getting started in publishing today, is there anything that you would do differently?

I wouldn't spend so much time on formal book signings. I think drop-in book signings are every bit as effective. Still my mistakes have taught me so much about this business that I'd hate to take anything back.

How do you view the advantages or disadvantages of self-publishing vs. traditional publishing?

I would never consider self-publishing. I think there was a time, maybe ten years ago, that self-published authors could sell enough books to attract the attention of a traditional publisher.

But now so many people are self-publishing books it's almost impossible to distinguish yourself. As a self-published author, you must hand-sell every copy of your book. There is no distribution, few opportunities to get press, and so much stigma attached to self-pubbed books. It takes a ton of work to market a self-published book. I think an author's efforts are far better utilized in doing what is necessary to find a traditional publisher, unless the author has a built-in audience for their work. (Like a doctor who does a lot of seminars.)

Do you have any favorite online resources or websites that you would like to recommend?

I think J. A. Konrath's blog A Newbie's Guide to Publishing is priceless: jakonrath.blogspot.com.

Also there's nothing like Publishers Marketplace to learn the ins and outs of the biz: publishersmarketplace.com.

What advice do you have for other authors?

Learn the business. Read extensively in your genre and not just best sellers. Pay particular attention to debut author releases. Keep up with the new deals by reading PublishersMarketplace.com. Remember that your novel is a product. Make it as marketable as possible without writing to the market.

Realize that writing is a craft that can take years to learn. Write every day even when you don't feel like it. Especially when you don't feel like it. That's the best way to become a writer.

CHAPTER 3

Setting Up Your Website

Launching a website can sound like an overwhelming task, but the good news is that it doesn't have to be. It also doesn't require that you take out a second mortgage on your home. Website hosting will probably cost you less than your monthly latte budget and there are affordable options for site design, too. This chapter will take you through the many options for launching a website that boosts your image without breaking the bank or your spirit.

Domain Names

Choosing a domain name is an important decision. Many authors simple use their pen names, such as StephanieChandler.com. But you might also want to register your site based on your book title or something related to the industry you are writing about.

To check if your domain is available, you can run a free search at smallbusiness.yahoo.com. If the domain is not available, consider using an acronym or abbreviation. If the name is available but you are not yet ready to launch your website, you may want to register the domain anyway so you don't lose it to someone else. It costs about $10 and gives you ownership of the name for one year, which you can later convert into an active website. When you register your domain name with Yahoo, you also have the ability to create a single page business card with your contact information. You can keep this active until you are ready to make your website live.

There are many free websites available from places like Yahoo's Geocities (geocities.yahoo.com). But if you use this service, you will not have your own domain name. Instead your URL will look something like this: *geocities.com/annieauthor.html*.

If you want to establish a professional presence on the Internet, you should invest in an affordable website hosting plan and your own domain name. Depending on the hosting provider and the features you require, it typically costs $10 to $20 per month to host a website. This is a small price to pay when the potential returns are so great.

Web Hosting Providers

A Web hosting provider serves as the headquarters for your website. A website actually resides within the large computer servers that are managed by the hosting provider. So though you will be able to update your website from your home or office computer, copies of your website files are stored with your hosting provider.

Because of this, choosing the right provider is an important decision. If your hosting provider's computers suffer an outage, then your website also goes out of commission. Depending on what kind of service agreement you have with your provider, your site could be down for hours, days, or even weeks. Some providers don't even back up their files so if they lose the data, it will be your responsibility to reload your website files back onto their servers—a painful and tedious process.

Keep this in mind when shopping for your hosting provider. It's best to ask lots of questions and review their service agreements. There are plenty of low-cost providers out there, just be sure they have some commitment to data backups, recovery, and "uptime." No computers are fail-safe so your provider may suffer an outage someday, but you need to know that your provider is committed to repairing problems in a reasonable amount of time. You also want to make sure you choose a company that is financially sound and will be there for the long haul.

I host my sites with Yahoo for a variety of reasons. The biggest reason is that I know that Yahoo isn't going anywhere. It's a big publicly-traded company which gives me confidence that when I wake up each morning, my websites will still be operating.

Yahoo's hosting packages start at just $12 per month: smallbusiness.yahoo.com. Their starter package includes hosting and up to 100 e-mail accounts that you can set up however you like. For example, you can have yourname@yourwebsite.com, webmaster@yourwebsite.com, customerservice@yourwebsite.com, etc. Yahoo also offers free site-building tools and templates that make it relatively easy to create a simple website operation.

If Yahoo isn't for you, there are plenty of other options. Network Solutions (NetworkSolutions.com) has a small business startup package for $35 per year that includes hosting and one e-mail address. The downside of having only one e-mail address is that you can't set up multiple mailboxes for customer service, sales, questions, etc. It just depends on your individual needs.

GoDaddy.com (GoDaddy.com) offers hosting for as little as $3.95 per month. Just be sure to weigh the value of less expensive hosting since some of these services charge for extras, like website security and traffic data (which you will want to have). A package that includes these options may be more cost effective.

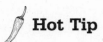 **Hot Tip**

Some hosting providers will actually require you to buy back your domain name if you miss a service payment. And I'm not just talking about the $10 per year registration fee. If you have a high traffic website and your payment lapses (perhaps your credit card expired before you could update the payment information), some providers will charge big bucks to sell you your domain back. Be sure to inquire about this policy when considering lesser-known hosting providers.

Website Design

The idea of designing a website from the ground up intimidates a lot of people, including me. Though I have experience with HTML (Hyper Text Markup Language, a language used to design websites), I admit that I don't have a good eye for design. But there is no shame in admitting our weaknesses and fortunately there are some simple and cost-effective solutions available.

There are scores of options when it comes to website design. You can do it yourself or hire someone to do it for you. It really depends on your needs and your skill set. I've tried a number of methods and my experiences have varied.

One option is to hire a website designer. Though you are likely to end up with a professional-looking site, this can be an expensive option. Also consider the long term. When someone else manages your site, you are at their mercy. Typically, you will have to pay extra for any changes to the data. Over the course of time, this can potentially add up to big money.

If you want to ultimately manage the data on your site yourself, you will want to find a designer who has the ability to set you up with a content management system. Another option, if you are so inclined, is to learn how to use DreamWeaver or another Web design tool. DreamWeaver is a very robust tool and is probably a good fit if you have a strong technical background.

Microsoft FrontPage is considered easier to use since many of the commands may be more intuitive if you're already using other Microsoft products. However, Microsoft has discontinued this product and is currently recommending their new product, Expresion Web. You can take a class at your local college or adult learning center to learn how to use any of these tools.

I still use Microsoft's tool to manage two of my three websites. When I originally opened my bookstore, I bartered with a local website designer and traded bookstore services for the original site design. The end result was adequate, though I never quite fell in love with the design. Since I was focused on so many other aspects of launching the new business, making significant changes to the website fell down the priority list.

Then something wonderful happened. I won a contest through *Entrepreneur* magazine and one of the prizes was a complete website redesign. In this case, the designer did an excellent job working with me to create the site that I wanted, and when it was finished, he handed over the files. This empowered me to manage the site myself without having to rely on the designer to make changes.

When I launched my business website (Business-InfoGuide.com), I discovered a fantastic innovation. For about $30, I purchased a preformatted website template for use with FrontPage. The entire foundation was there, including slick drop-down menus, a variety of Web page layouts and a professional looking theme. All I had to do was fill in the content, make a few tweaks, and I was up and running. It was the best $30 I've ever spent. There are numerous businesses that offer website templates. I found mine at TheTemplateStore.com and couldn't be happier with the choice I made. In fact, I also purchased a template for my writing business (ProPublishingServices.com).

I actually used a free template to design my initial writer site. The only difference is that it was a free template provided by my hosting provider. Since I knew my design skills were lacking and I only needed a simple static site, I decided to use Yahoo's free Site Builder tool and one of their preformatted templates. The tool is user-friendly and I was able to get the website up and running in just one evening.

Moving Forward

The decision to launch a website for the first time can seem overwhelming so take your time. You may want to discuss these options with other writers whom you know. Find out how they got their sites up and running. If you are particularly fond of an associate's site, you may want to ask for a referral to the designer.

Submit to Search Engines

The search engines won't know your website exists if you don't tell them about it. In fact, it can take many months before your site shows up in Google, Yahoo and the other search engines.

As soon as your site is up and running, be sure to submit your link to the major search engines. Each search engine has a simple process for submitting your Web link for inclusion that usually involves filling out a brief submission form.

Visit each of the major search engine home pages (Yahoo, Google, AOL, MSN) and locate instructions for submitting your site for consideration. You can usually find these near the bottom of the page. Even after submitting, it can still take weeks for your site to get approved and appear in the search engines so it is critical that you submit your link as soon as possible.

Search Engine Optimization

There are entire books written on the subject of search engine optimization, also commonly known as SEO. SEO is what you do to improve your rankings with the search engines. So when someone searches for "free kittens," the search engine lists the results based on a variety of factors for each website that contains the term "free kittens."

To complicate matters further, each search engine has different criteria for how it ranks Web pages—and the criteria gets more sophisticated each year. Google has complex algorithms that it uses, although the company is open about sharing the details. You can visit Google's site, or any of the search engines, to find their latest suggestions for optimizing your site. For now I'll share with you some of the basics that you should be doing at a minimum.

Words Matter

The search engines "crawl" websites and scan words and phrases looking for patterns in the content. In order to get the most exposure for your website, the keywords and terms you use should be carefully chosen. So, if you have a book about politics, but don't use the word "politics" in various places throughout your site, the search engines won't be able to find you when Web surfers search for politics or books about politics.

Every Web page has three important elements that should be addressed:

Keywords: When building Web page content, one of the most important SEO strategies involves including relevant keywords. When defining keywords and phrases for each of your Web pages, consider the search terms that your target audience would use to find you. For example, if you are the author of a low-carbohydrate diet book, your keywords would likely include "low carbohydrate," "diet," "diet book," "lose weight," "weight loss," and other similar terms.

Jim Tendick, search engine optimization expert and owner of ebizboosters.com, recommends conducting some research first. "It really starts by guessing what words people are typing in [the search engines] that are related to your book," said Tendick.

He recommends leveraging the free trial service from wordtracker.com. Here you can type in keywords and generate a list of related terms that the analyzer has determined are most popular with Web surfers. Each keyword and phrase is ranked based on popularity.

Another way to determine popularity is to type a keyword phrase in to Google and see how many results are returned. If there are 10,000,000 pages with that phrase, it is going to be nearly impossible to end up in the top ten results on the search engine. But even with a high number of pages returned, Tendick says there is still hope. "Believe it or not, 80,000 is my comfortable cutoff. Using optimization strategies, we have been able to get our clients listed in the top ten over and over again."

Tendick says that the key is to identify no more than two or three keyword phrases per page for your website. "We see this a lot with Realtors who try to list the twenty cities that they serve on one page. This just dilutes the results." A better strategy is to build additional pages into the site and spread out the concentration of keywords and phrases.

Once you have identified your keywords, they should be naturally included in the content on your Web page. Also important, they should be listed in the meta tags for the page. Meta tags are part of the Web page code that tells the search engines what the page is all about.

Title: This is seen at the top of the visitor's Web browser and in the search results displayed by the search engines. Nothing makes me cringe more than simply seeing the word "Home" listed as the title of a Web page. Though you are limited to the number of characters a title can have, it should reflect the vital details of the page.

Using the diet book example, the title for the home page might be, "Wayne Writer, Author of *Low Carbohydrate Diet Solutions Book*."

Tendick advises that your title should have no more than 65 characters. Also, it should not only include your relevant keyword phrases for the page but it should also entice browsers to click since the title is listed in the results on the search engine listing.

Description: The description for each page on a website is also read and displayed by the search engines. Again, this is a vitally important place to list the crucial details and keywords for the page.

For example, the diet book might have this description: "Official Site of Wayne Writer, author of *Low Carbohydrate Diet Solutions*, a weight loss book that gets results."

Accidental Success Story

Barry Schoenborn, owner of WVS: The Technical Writing Company, discovered some accidental success in his company's website placement on Google. By naturally using his company name throughout his home page (wvswrite.com), his site is currently ranked in the number four position on Google when searching for "technical writing company." This is evidence that keywords matter, even when your efforts aren't intentional.

Real-World Example

Here is what the code looks like on my website page that promotes my second book (businessinfoguide.com/infopreneur-book.htm):

```
<title>Book: From Entrepreneur to Infopreneur by Stephanie
Chandler</title>
<meta name="keywords" content="infopreneur, information
products, info products, e-books, special reports, teleseminars, mul-
tiple streams of income, products, information, publishing, books,
how to, infopreneur marketing, e-books, Stephanie Chandler">
<meta name="description" content="Business Book: From
Entrepreneur to Infopreneur: Make Money With Books, E-books
and Information Products by Stephanie Chandler. Learn how you
can generate multiple streams of income as an infopreneur by cre-
ating and selling information products. ">
```

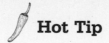 **Hot Tip**

You can view the keywords on virtually any Web page from your browser. This can be very handy in understanding what words and phrases your competitors are using. To do this with Internet Explorer, display a Web page and click on View > Source. The HTML source code will display in a text file and near the top you will see the title, description and keywords listed in the text.

Links = Popularity

One of the quickest ways to build credibility with the search engines is to have your website link listed on as many relevant high-traffic websites as possible. The search engines consider this important criteria that demonstrates that your site is popular because so many other sites are referencing it on their pages.

The challenge for you is to find ways to get your link listed on as many sites as possible. Include your link with every single post you make online to forums, blogs, etc. Also, update your profile for any trade organizations that you belong to. Don't forget to update your profiles on Amazon.com, Yahoo, MySpace.com, Classmates.com, and every other site to which you are a member.

SEO expert Jim Tendick advocates the use of anchored links. An anchored link is a link that is embedded into text on a page. For example, when you see "Click here for more details" and the phrase has a hyperlink that takes you to a Web page, that is an anchored link.

Ideally your anchored links should include the keyword phrases that match those listed on the target Web page. So if another website references your "Low Carbohydrate Diet Book" and embeds the link back to your home page, that holds much more value with the search engines that simply list the link to your home page.

It takes time to get your link out there, so develop as many strategies as you can. This is one major benefit of publishing articles online since the more your article is syndicated to other websites, the more your link is published (more on publishing articles coming up).

Content Is King

One of the worst things you can do is let your website become a stale sales brochure. The search engines give rank to websites that change content frequently. By simply making a few changes on your home page periodically, the search engines will consider your site to be more relevant.

In order to keep your website in the highest regard with the search engines, you should be adding or changing content on a regular basis. Some website owners do this by maintaining a news page or by adding news and events to the home page. Another way to increase relevance is to make a habit of adding new content such as articles or related industry information.

There are some additional benefits to adding content frequently. First, you give your site visitors even more information to enjoy and a reason to come back again and again. Second, you give the search engines more reasons to find your site.

For example, if you have a book about California wines, you could add articles and reviews about specific types of wine. When an Internet surfer types in a particular brand of wine that you feature in content on your site, they are likely to land on your page provided there isn't too much competition for that particular search phrase.

One of the most popular pages on BusinessInfoGuide.com is an article that profiles two shoe store owners in San Francisco. As it turns out, there isn't much competition online for terms like "open a shoe store." So visitors find the article on BusinessInfoGuide.com, discover the site as a valuable resource for entrepreneurs, and hopefully sign up for the electronic newsletter and ultimately purchase some of my books and products.

Paid Search Engine Placement

You may want to consider paying to have your website placed at the top of search engines. One of the more popular providers for paid placement is Overture (which is now run by Yahoo.): searchmarketing.yahoo.com.

Known as pay-per-click, this service allows you to bid on keywords and phrases in order to have your site listed in the top three or five search results. Bids can start as low as $.10 per click and popular keyword phrases can cost several dollars depending on how much bidding competition there is for each keyword or phrase.

For example, I have a pay-per-click campaign setup with relevant keywords to promote my e-book called "How to Start and Run a Used Bookstore." Since I don't have much competition in this space, I pay just a few cents per click and visitors are taken directly to the sales page for this book. Many of the clicks to my site convert to book sales and make my investment completely worthwhile.

For my business startup guide, the high cost of clicks doesn't make this method worthwhile for this particular book. There is simply too much competition for keywords related to business startup and as a result, pay-per-click rates are as high as $1 or more per click. In this case, I choose to focus my online marketing efforts elsewhere for this particular title.

Google AdWords (adwords.google.com) is another option for paid search engine advertising. Google places your ad and link to your site on other websites based on keywords you specify. For example, if you have a pastry recipe book, your ad would likely be placed on cooking-related sites. With AdWords you also pay for each click through to your site.

The challenge with these pay-for-placement services is that you are paying *only for a click through to your site*, not when you've actually sold something or gained a new customer. The costs for these services can add up quickly. You do have the option to set a budget so that if you're only willing to spend $50 per month, your ads will be temporarily suspended once you've reached your budget limit and will start again the next month.

If you have a niche topic or want to drive traffic to your website, it may be worthwhile to test the pay-per-click advertising model. With some testing of different keyword combinations and persuasive ad copy, this strategy has the ability to draw traffic quickly. Just remember that you can draw the best traffic in the world, but if you're not converting that traffic to sales, then it's time to evaluate your sales pitch.

Boost Exposure with a Blog

There has been tremendous buzz around the benefit of blogs. A blog essentially works like an online diary, allowing the owner to post entries on a regular basis. Some people post daily, others post once or twice a week. Search engine optimization experts recommend posting entries at least three times per week for the best search engine placement.

Blogs work best when they focus on a specific topic. For example, if you are the author of a local history book, you could post interesting historical facts and details from around the region. You could also interview other local historians and post the results on your blog.

The belief in the Internet community has been that blogs are more quickly indexed by search engines, partly because there is plenty of new content being added on a regular basis. Many authors boast tremendous success from their blogs. Some use a blog as an enhancement to their primary website and some are building notoriety by simply hosting an interesting or controversial blog.

Linda Formichelli and Diana Burrell, authors of "The Renegade Writer," share the duties of posting to their popular blog for writers: therenegadewriter.com. The result is that they have created a valuable resource for the writing community and have built a loyal fan base.

There are pros and cons to hosting a blog. Here are some to consider:

Pros

- ✓ Blogs are relatively easy to set up.
- ✓ Most blogging programs are free or very low-cost.
- ✓ Blogs may be indexed by search engines frequently which means your ranking can improve quickly, making it easier for new visitors to find you.
- ✓ If you enjoy writing and sharing details related to your book(s), a blog can be a fun and creative tool for promotion.
- ✓ If you want to become a recognized expert in your field, a blog is a quick credibility-builder.

Cons

- ✓ You have to find plenty of topics to write about or else posting regularly can be frustrating after awhile.

✓ It can be time consuming to manage a blog.

✓ If you're already too busy, this could begin to feel like an obligation.

When I first started my blog (businessinfoguide.com/blog), I wasn't sure what to write about. Over time I grew so frustrated, I ended up putting it on hold for several months. It so happens that I had also just had a baby and was too overwhelmed to handle many of my regular commitments.

But when I reunited with my blog, I had a new outlook. I had also learned a few tricks. Blog entries don't need to be long because readers tend to scan and don't want to read long-winded posts. Just one to three paragraphs is ideal. I also realized that I could post several entries at once and set a schedule for when they would publish on the site (typically Monday, Wednesday and Friday).

Most importantly, I got a rhythm going with content. On days when I feel inspired to write, I try to hammer out several posts at once. I also realized that I could post guest submissions from readers of my newsletter and also include book reviews, quick tips or links to other useful websites. Once I stopped viewing my blog as an obligation, it became a fun and valuable promotion tool.

Setting Up Your Blog

Your Web service provider may have a blog service available that you can integrate into your existing website. If not, you can get started with blogger.com, wordpress.com or typepad.com.

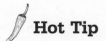 **Hot Tip**

Even if you don't have a blog, you can certainly read other people's blogs. You can also post comments on blogs and include a link back to your website. Not only will other blog readers see your post, but the blog owner might just be compelled to check out your site. You never know what kind of alliance might be formed as a result.

Promoting Your Blog

Resources for bloggers abound and you can maximize the exposure for your blog by listing it in blog directories. These directories allow blog readers to search for blogs based on topics of interest to them. Here are some directories to check out:

- ✓ answers.com/main/new_blogger.jsp
- ✓ blogcatalog.com
- ✓ blog-directory.org
- ✓ bloghub.com
- ✓ blogrankings.com
- ✓ blogflux.com
- ✓ bloggernity.com
- ✓ blogsforsmallbusiness.com
- ✓ globeofblogs.com/register.php
- ✓ dir.yahoo.com/news_and_media/blogs

Additional Blog Resources

- ✓ bloggersblog.com—Interesting news and information on blogging trends
- ✓ weblogs.about.com—About.com's guide to blogs

Author Interview

Author: Diana Ennen

Most recent book: *Office Ready Virtual Assistant Solution Pack*

Total # of books published: Two by trade publishers, six self-published

Website: virtualwordpublishing.com

What is your book about?

My book is mainly on how to start and operate a successful virtual assistant business. It takes you step by step through the startup stage, setting up your business for success, obtaining clients and marketing, and most importantly, how to set up your business to keep it successful.

What led you to publish the book?

Starting a business really takes a lot of knowledge and skills, but it also takes a lot of motivation. In writing my books, I wanted to provide that motivation, and I truly believe I have. Plus with years of experience in being a virtual assistant myself, I knew things that worked and things that didn't. I wanted to help others avoid the costly mistakes I made but also reap the benefits when something I tried worked.

How has being an author changed or improved your life personally or professionally?

Being an author gave me so much self-confidence. I always wanted to write and when it finally happened and I was published,

I was beyond thrilled. Initially I didn't think it mattered if I sold many books, as being an author was enough. However, through the years I realized I liked those royalty checks coming in and that you can make a good income from writing. What I discovered was that anyone can do this if they really have a passion for it.

Professionally it has helped me considerably as well. It totally established me as expert and the one to come to in the virtual assistant industry. Also, because I offer publicity and marketing, I believe knowing that I'm an author helps potential publicity clients to see that not only can I help them with getting publicity, but I can help them write their material as well.

What online marketing methods have worked best for you?

I get my best results with sending out articles and press releases. The key for me was to do this regularly. I believe what happens with a lot of authors is that they send out an article every few months and expect results. For me, by sending out articles and releases frequently, my name is constantly out there. I will often hear, "You are everywhere." I love that as then I know it's working.

Also, I cohost a podcast with Jill Hart of Christian Work at Home Moms that has been very successful. I think when people can hear your message as well as read it, that adds to your credibility substantially.

Do you have a favorite off-line book marketing strategy?

I do have a favorite off-line book marketing strategy and that is to always carry my books with me. For example, I also published a children's book entitled *Zip, Burp and Hula*, which is just a delightful book. I take the book with me everywhere I go as it fits right in my purse. I have been able on numerous occasions to give it to a child who perhaps is restless waiting at a doctor's office or in line at the post office, or at my kids' school events. That almost always leads to more book sales. I have my business card stapled to the book, and I've even gotten clients this way. It does cost a little, but the results have been very worth it.

I also attend business networking events and because I have a book on how to start a business, that has been very successful for me as well.

Do you own a business?

Yes I do, Virtual Word Publishing. I offer publicity and marketing. I also market my own books. I've been in business since 1985 and absolutely love what I do.

Has being an author helped your business in any way? How?

It has helped me considerably. When people see the success I have with marketing my own books, they feel more confident entrusting me with their publicity. Plus, since I offer virtual assistant coaching as well, having written my books, virtual assistants hopefully can see that I know what I'm talking about and come to me for guidance in starting their business.

If you were just getting started in publishing today, is there anything that you would do differently?

I think the main thing I would change would be to do more research on the publisher before I sign on to get published. I would look to see what other books they have published and how successful those are and I would find out what happens after they publish the book and exactly how active you can be or need to be in the publicity of the book. Also, go on publishers' forums and see if they are active on them. Not all publishers are on these forums, however, some are and you can get a sense of how they run their publishing business by their comments.

Sometimes I feel authors are so amazed when a publishing company accepts them, that they just sign up and don't do their research. You want to make sure the company you choose will stand behind you and your book for the long haul.

How do you view the advantages or disadvantages of self-publishing vs. traditional publishing?

I absolutely love self-publishing. I love being in control so I can ensure the success of my book. I really like the time factor. With a traditional publisher, everything is on their time clock, but when you publish yourself, you control that.

I feel if you do your research, you can avoid many of the disadvantages of being self-published.

Do you have any favorite online resources or websites that you would like to recommend?

Nancy Cleary has a fabulous free class on publishing: wymacpublishing.com.

Also, Irene Watson of Reader's View: readersview.com. They offer book reviews, interviews, etc. They are absolutely fabulous and give one-on-one attention to every author.

I also like the self-publishers Yahoo group: Self-Publishing-@yahoogroups.com.

What advice do you have for other authors?

Enjoy the journey. If you have fun and don't stress while writing and promoting your book you will be all the more successful. Also, realize that writing a book is just the beginning. The real job begins after it is published and you begin to market it. However, keep in mind that can be just as exciting. Also, write on something you know about and are passionate about.

CHAPTER 4

Website Enhancement Tools

Once you have established the foundation for your website, it's time to take it up a notch. Your site can be more than just a portal of information—it can generate profits. This chapter covers tools and tricks for making the most of your website.

Making Your Books Available for Purchase

You are quite likely losing money if you don't offer a way for website visitors to purchase your books from your website. I have been one of those shoppers who stumbled across an author's site and discovered a fascinating book only to find that there was no way to place an order. Sure I could log on to Amazon.com or BN.com, search for the book and place the order myself, but I would have to be pretty motivated to take those additional steps. Remember, Internet users have short attention spans. Everything about your website should be quick and easy.

This chapter includes information for setting up a shopping cart system on your website. But if you don't want to deal with shipping your own books (which is perfectly understandable), the easiest solution is to provide a direct link to your book's page on one or more online bookstores.

Some authors prefer to support independent stores while others simply leverage the mainstream stores. Either way, as long as you are providing visitors an easy way to place an order, you are increasing the chances of reeling in a new reader.

Another option is to sign up for the associates program with Amazon.com. This program allows you to earn a commission when you recommend books to others for purchase. You can generate a unique link to your book (or any other book if you are so inclined) and make it available from your website. This program allows you to track the number of copies sold each month via your website and Amazon will pay you for any additional books the shopper purchases at the same time.

There is no cost to join, though you are required to fill out an application. Once approved, you will be able to login to your associates account and generate links or review sales reports. Amazon pays commission on a monthly basis.

To sign up, visit: affiliate-program.amazon.com/gp/associates/join.

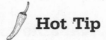 **Hot Tip**

Don't have a fax line? Consider investing in an electronic fax with a service such as efax.com. You can receive faxes for free with their basic service (you will be assigned a long-distance number) or for a fee of around $15 per month, you can obtain a local fax number. Faxes are delivered to your e-mail inbox so you can receive them from anywhere you can access e-mail.

Shopping Carts and Payment Processing

If you plan to sell your book(s) on your website, you will need to set up a shopping cart and have the ability to accept credit cards. There are dozens of shopping cart programs available depending on your needs. Your website host may offer one at no additional charge. Alternately, you can search the Internet for shopping cart software or use one of the vendors listed here.

Paypal

If you have a limited number of books or you simply want to test the waters, Paypal provides a quick and easy way to add a shopping cart to your website. This wholly-owned subsidiary of eBay is primarily a payment processing service. Once you sign up for a free Paypal account, you can quickly create shopping cart buttons to insert on your Web pages.

When a customer makes a purchase, Paypal takes the buyer through the payment process and delivers an e-mail receipt when payment is complete. As the merchant, you receive notification via e-mail that your product has sold, along with the buyer's shipping information.

Like all merchant card processors, Paypal charges a fee per transaction. Their rates are based on the amount of transactions processed each month and are slightly higher than a standard merchant card processor. But unlike merchant card processors, Paypal doesn't charge a monthly fee nor does it set any minimum transaction requirements.

Paypal used to require shoppers to register before it would process an order, but this is no longer the case. Today orders processed through Paypal are comparable to most other online shopping experiences.

As an added bonus, Paypal now offers a virtual terminal service which allows you to accept credit cards remotely. For example, you can accept cards at speaking engagements and other off-site book signing events.

1ShoppingCart

If you intend to sell a large volume of books and products, 1ShoppingCart.com provides a comprehensive online shopping cart system. Depending on the level of service you choose, you can create shopping cart buttons, offer special discounts or sale prices on your books, create gift certificates, automate e-mail delivery with auto-responders and deliver e-books securely.

You can also use 1ShoppingCart's merchant account provider to process credit cards or integrate the shopping cart with a different merchant processor. Separate transaction and monthly fees apply so be sure to check the website for the latest fee schedule.

Payloadz

If you plan to sell electronic downloads such as e-books or MP3 files, Payloadz.com allows you to set up shopping cart buttons and automates the delivery of electronic products. The service is integrated with Paypal so payment transactions are easily processed through your Paypal account.

Payloadz offers two types of fee schedules. You can choose between a standard 15 percent transaction fee with no additional monthly fee, or you can pay a flat monthly rate. The monthly rates are based on the amount of storage space required to host your electronic files and the total transactions processed in a thirty-day period. Visit the Payloadz website for the fee structure.

As an added benefit, Payloadz hosts its own eBay store so you can list your electronic products for sale on eBay. You can also setup an affiliate program and offer commissions to others who sell your products.

Yahoo!

If you would like to create a custom online store with the added exposure of being listed in Yahoo's massive shopping site, Yahoo Merchant Solutions may be the answer. For under $40 per month, Yahoo's starter program includes Web hosting, up to 100 e-mail accounts and the tools to set up your shopping cart. Yahoo also charges a transaction fee for each sale under this package.

Yahoo stores integrate with most merchant card processors or you can sign up for an account with their partner, Paymentech (paymentech.net). Yahoo also offers incentives for signing up such as credits toward search engine marketing services and discounts on services from their partners. For more information, visit smallbusiness.yahoo.com/merchant.

Affiliate Marketing

Once your website shopping cart service is in full swing, you can generate more sales by offering your own affiliate program. These programs allow other authors and businesses to sell your books and products on a commission basis. For example, you could set up an affiliate program and offer other online merchants a 25 percent commission for each of your books that they sell.

Most of the online shopping cart services allow you to set up affiliate links for your business partners. If you're using Paypal or another service that doesn't provide the ability to set up affiliate accounts, you can set one up through clickbank.com or paydotcom.com.

If you do offer an affiliate program for your products, make it as easy as possible for your sellers. Provide them with full product descriptions and high-quality graphic images. Don't forget to offer enough commission to make their efforts worthwhile.

 **Hot Tip**

It's a good idea to have a printable order form that site visitors can either fax or mail. Not everyone is comfortable with transmitting their credit card across the Internet, so to capture all sales, make sure to have an order form available.

Marketing with Audio

Have you noticed that more and more websites have audio built right in to the pages? Some start talking as you land on the page, while others offer a control box where you can decide if you want to listen to the recorded message.

I have yet to fall in love with this technology. In fact, I am completely turned off by a website if it starts yelling at me the minute I land on the page. It can be quite startling, especially for people like me who like to surf the Internet at 2:00 A.M.

However, we all learn differently. Some learn better visually and others learn by listening. When you add audio recordings to a website you cover both bases. You can use audio clips to introduce yourself, describe a special offer or even read an excerpt from your book. New technology makes it easy to create recordings and embed them right into your website and many believe that this is a great way to let site visitors get to know you.

You can run an Internet search for "audio recording software" and find dozens of choices. One product that I have used is Audio Acrobat (audioacrobat.com). This is a nifty subscription-based tool that allows you to quickly create recordings and save them in MP3 format using a basic phone line. It's quick and easy to use and the price is reasonable.

Marketing with Video

One of the most interesting online marketing opportunities to arise in recent years comes from the proliferation of video. Much attention has been brought to this medium thanks to YouTube.com, a free service where subscribers can upload short videos for public viewing. YouTube made waves in mainstream news when Google acquired the company in 2006 for over $1.6 billion in stock.

Video sharing is viral marketing at its best. Viral marketing is a term used to describe marketing that takes on a life of its own, typically through some form of word-of-mouth. For example, I recently received an e-mail forwarded by a friend. The message included a short video clip featuring a stand-up comic giving a funny talk about her experience at a nail salon.

This video turned into a viral marketing campaign because people were spontaneously compelled to share it with others. Even smarter, the comedian listed her website across the bottom of the screen throughout her entire performance.

If your book has the potential for any type of visual presentation, a video could be in order. Take a look at some of the most popular videos on YouTube on any given day. The most viewed choices tend to be funny or controversial.

In another example, Judson Laipply, a self-proclaimed "Inspirational Comedian," produced a short video called "The Evolution of Dance." This is a performance that he gives at the end of his comedy shows and includes an ensemble of music and a live demonstration of a variety of dance moves that progress from the Twist to the Sprinkler to break dancing.

This production was so funny that it shot to the top of the YouTube watch list and ultimately caught the attention of producers at *The Today Show*. Laipply was invited to perform his dance ensemble on live television. Can you imagine what that has done for his career?

In addition to uploading videos to YouTube and other video sharing services, more and more Internet marketers are using video clips on their websites. Whether a video starts playing when the page opens, or a control panel option allows visitors to push play (my personal preference), there are many ways to maximize exposure with this medium:

✓ Let website visitors get to know you.
✓ Deliver an interesting message in a unique way (humor is always good).
✓ Demonstrate your speaking skills.
✓ Give a reading from your book.
✓ Capture testimonials or reviews from your readers.
✓ Demonstrate a concept from your book.
✓ Provide an entertaining performance that complements your book.
✓ Sell a video as a product.
✓ Send video clips to TV and film producers.
✓ Interview subjects from your book.

The list goes on and on. Video is so mainstream today that many major companies are now streaming videos of their corporate meetings and events and day care centers are setting up Web cams to give parents an added level of comfort.

Sue Peppers, founder of Peppers.tv, a video production company, says that there are many ways authors can leverage video to build an audience. For example, she once worked with an aspiring author who had plans to publish a book. The writer didn't have a platform or ready-made audience for the book and wanted to find a way to leverage video and her website to build an audience.

The writer was also a cancer survivor and marathon runner who had been featured on a variety of news programs. The team at Peppers.tv took her many media clips along with video from the writer's speaking engagements, and edited it all together. "It was remarkably powerful," said Peppers, "and it helped viewers get to know [the writer] and tell her story."

Another way to leverage video is during speaking engagements. Public speaking is the number one fear for Americans and if your knees quiver at the platform, video can come to the rescue. According to Peppers, "If you can't talk because you're afraid you're going to freak out, instead you can walk in, introduce yourself and play a great video. Leave ten minutes available at the end for questions and you're done."

The visual impact of video to tell a story can enhance any presentation. Preview clips can be added to your website. Authors can also produce video demonstrations that complement topics from a book or create entertaining short movie clips to illustrate works of fiction.

Though you can attempt to produce your own video, keep in mind that a subpar production could potentially hurt more than it helps. "There's a psychological thing that happens when consumers see professional marketing materials," says Peppers. "A good video can make you look trustworthy and professional."

Peppers adds that it's not unlike when someone hands you a business card that is obviously homemade. "It changes your opinion about the level of professionalism of that person. On the other hand, a high-quality card on excellent paper makes a great impression."

The Internet makes it remarkably easy and affordable to make videos available. If you want to produce a television show, it can cost millions to make it generally available on traditional television networks. But you can host it on a website for less than the cost of your monthly gasoline bill.

Video Is the Future

Technology experts report that video has a thriving future on the Internet. While today the search engines are only able to read text, soon they will be indexing video and graphic images. And as more and more users migrate to high speed Internet, bandwidth issues are minimized.

Additional Video Sharing Services

✓ video.google.com
✓ video.yahoo.com
✓ blip.tv
✓ ourmedia.org
✓ vsocial.com
✓ clipshack.com

Video Education Resources

✓ Peppers.tv provides video production services for projects large and small: Peppers.tv.
✓ John Easton hosts a comprehensive and interesting blog on the topic of video production: eastonsweb.wordpress.com.

Author Interview

Author: Dan S. Kennedy

Most recent books: *No B.S. DIRECT Marketing For NON-Direct Marketing Businesses* and *No. B.S. Wealth Attraction For Entrepreneurs*

Total # of books published: Eleven by trade publishers, eight self-published

websites: NoBSBooks.com and DanKennedy.com

What are your books about?

The NO B.S. book series (five titles, the sixth is scheduled for release in 2008) presents a combination of street-smart, experience-based, rather radical and controversial "No BS," NO academic theory, NO warm-n-fuzzy strategies specifically for entrepreneurs along with my own philosophy, opinions and life experiences. The Ultimate series ("Ultimate Marketing Plan" and "Ultimate Sales Letter") are narrowly-focused, step-by-step how-to manuals.

What led you to publish the books?

To be frank, I publish for promotion first, profit second, primarily as one of many means of both brand building and direct lead generation in support of the companies I'm associated with (I edit four different company newsletters, create information products, conduct conferences, etc.). In short, I view books as an advertising media.

How has being an author changed or improved your life personally or professionally?

Not much in and of itself—and I think that the person hooked on the fantasy that merely being a published author will change everything for them is in for a very unpleasant time of it.

The books utilized in context of many other self-promotion media, activities and tools integrated with online and off-line marketing, manual labor like speaking, etc., well, that has made me financially independent and a "brand name" and "personality" of substantial continuing value.

The books have, at different times and in different ways, provided credibility and celebrity, entry to media that would otherwise have been denied, and a series of very specific, orchestrated opportunities that, again, would be more difficult to create absent the books. For example, when three books came out in 2007, we orchestrated promotion to our e-mail mailing lists, affiliates' mailing lists and media that generated over 15,000 people on a teleseminar.

What online marketing methods have worked best for you?

The author without a promotional platform is at huge disadvantage. Early, writing books helped build mine; now I can be virtually assured of 10,000 to 20,000 copies being sold quickly via my own platform that includes newsletters, e-zines, websites reaching from 15,000 to 150,000 that I control, plus Glazer-Kennedy Insider's Circle affiliates, chapters in more than 90 cities, over 50 niched newsletters that use my content, and a small number of key media contacts I've cultivated. Beyond that, I have personally found traditional approaches to publicity, publicists, book signings and working with bookstores unproductive.

I typically buy full-page and fractional ads in at least five relevant national magazines with my own money to drive book sales; I make myself available to do teleseminars to appropriate business audiences, and I strategically involve others with their own promotion platforms. In fact, I consider that even when deciding who to mention or relate a story about in the book.

Through our company, Bill Glazer and I work together on online promotion and utilize the Internet extensively. As an example, a visit to NoBSBooks.com will reveal video interviews with me and Kristi Frank from *The Apprentice* [Donald Trump's television show] about my books. I hired Kristi for this, to use in magazine ads and for personal appearances. That same site has free chapters and other resources, as well as links to other sites.

We also work aggressively, with my publishers and independently, to leverage Amazon.com, BarnesandNoble.com, 800-CEO-READ and other online and direct distribution. I also push my publishers—and rely on them—to get superior distribution. For example, my Ultimate titles are stocked and sold in FedEx/Kinkos stores as well as bookstores. The NO BS titles have been featured in special displays at Borders and on end-caps at Barnes and Noble.

By far and away, the most effective media used to promote my books is the Internet. Because of the absence of cost limitations for websites and e-mail, the speed of e-mail, and thus the ease of getting influencers, co-promoters and affiliates to send mass e-mails to their lists on my behalf, we're able to reach hundreds of thousands of qualified people with high probability of interest in these titles quickly, efficiently, and affordably. To achieve the same reach in a short period of time via other means would be prohibitively expensive and time consuming.

I do think authors underestimate how much online activity and how many people have to be touched multiple times to drive book sales. My own admittedly unscientific best guess is that you might sell 1,000 books for every one million online touches (delivered e-mails, visits to a site, etc.). This is a very cluttered environment. E-mail nondelivery is a huge, growing problem. It takes an enormous amount of activity and viral buzz to move a small number of books.

Are there any methods you have used that haven't yielded impressive results?

As I said, trying to work with retail booksellers in various ways—including, once, a weekly promotional newsletter faxed to every independent bookstore in the U.S. and Canada—has been consistently disappointing.

Do you have a favorite off-line book marketing strategy?

My time is extremely valuable, so actually buying magazine advertising is a bargain for me, is reasonably effective, and has side-effect value. The most effective thing is working with other influencers, speakers, newsletter publishers, etc. To get the books reviewed, excerpted, and promoted is #1. I also distribute "free Kennedy content" to nearly 1,000 publishers via a program provided to members by [my] Information Marketing Association (info-marketing.org).

Do you own a business?

In recent years, I have sold my businesses but remain connected. The biggest, Glazer-Kennedy Insider's Circle, has over 20,000 member-subscribers, over ninety chapters in cities throughout the U.S. and Canada, five different coaching programs, two major annual conferences, three monthly newsletters and a substantial catalog business—all focused on delivering my advertising, marketing, sales and business strategies to entrepreneurs, sales professionals and self-employed professionals like dentists, chiropractors, attorneys, etc.

There are two other smaller publishing businesses. For many years I spoke professionally at seventy-plus events a year but I've nearly ceased that by choice to avoid the travel. I have a group of about fifty private coaching and consulting clients, and do a considerable amount of direct-response copywriting for ads, direct-mail campaigns, online media and TV infomercials. An entry point for people curious about businesses is a free gift trial membership to the Insider's Circle, available at DanKennedy.com.

Has being an author helped your business in any way?

Being a published author of books, published by good publishers, with good distribution, is definitely helpful in many ways. There is, as I said earlier, support for me and my #1 brand, "NO B.S.," direct lead generation, producing members, consulting clients, etc.; and access to valuable promotional opportunities that might otherwise be unavailable. I also think I connect on a deeper and more thorough level with people through my books than through more temporary and more brief media, like newsletters. I can tell you that people who come to us through these books are better, more valuable customers than those arriving via all other sources.

If you were just getting started in publishing today, is there anything that you would do differently?

I'm always learning, so there are certainly things we did better in promoting the most recent books than the year before for those books, and I hope we'll be even smarter and more effective in 2008 with the next two. The two biggest things I fully embrace now that I did not fully understand when I was first published in 1991 are one: how incredibly ignorant and inept the publishers are about marketing, and two: that the book itself is nearly irrelevant and financially valueless, unless used as a means of carrying out a comprehensive, sophisticated promotion that drives people into a single place—what we call a *marketing funnel*—that converts them to customers giving you money repeatedly or continuously. Few authors understand this. Many even resent its reality.

How do you view the advantages or disadvantages of self-publishing vs. traditional publishing?

Both have virtues and evils, and rather than rehash those—as I'm sure others in your book discuss them—I'll point out that I have never considered this an either/or proposition. I have done both simultaneously and continuously for more than fifteen years.

Self-publishing gives you profit and flexibility; trade publishing gives you promotion and distribution. Just as example, I have a little book titled *Why Do I Always Have To Sit Next To The Farting Cat?* designed to be bought in bulk by certain kinds of companies and given to their customers. It's published by Kennedy/Lillo Associates (PeteThePrinter.com). We've sold over 200,000 copies. It's what I call a viral product, published for a very special purpose, with nominal profit, but as a promotion tool.

I don't think all my trade-published titles *together* have sold 200,000 copies. But their presence in bookstores serves different and important purposes. One made *Inc. Magazine's* list of 100 best business books, a "bragging right" I've gotten and get a lot of mileage from—and that would never occur for the cat book or hardly any self-published title. My NO B.S. books published by Entrepreneur Press have had months of airport bookstore distribution, reaching ideal customers for me—and that kind of distribution is virtually out of reach for self-published books.

What advice do you have for other authors?

Don't waste your time *just* being an author. Use writing, being published and publishing as media and means for developing a full-fledged, comprehensive business that has legs and longevity, and gives you direct relationship with customers. Few books will support you in style for life. A few thousand good customers eager to hear from you, come to events with you, get coaching from you, etc. will support you in a millionaire lifestyle, for life. I have found this to be unwelcome advice by most authors and virtually all would-be others. But since you asked.

$$\boxed{\textbf{CHAPTER 5}}$$

Building Your Expert Status

One of the quickest ways to build notoriety and sell more books is to become a recognized expert in your field. If you have a special degree or certification, you have built-in credentials and should seize every opportunity to exploit them. But even without a piece of paper that certifies you as an expert, you can start by simply claiming your expert status.

Everyone is an expert at something. Whether you are passionate about martial arts, have golfed on dozens of courses around the world or you're the person your friends come to for parenting advice, you know more about your favorite subject than the average person.

Rachael Ray is one of the most famous experts around today. Though she is the host of several cooking-related television shows, runs a self-titled magazine and has authored numerous books, Ray has never received any professional chef training. That didn't stop the powers that be at the Food Network or Oprah's production company from taking notice. Ray's down-to-earth style and knack for transforming regular food into better-than-regular food has made her a wealthy icon and a food expert with worldwide recognition.

But There Are Already Other Experts

Many authors believe that because there are others already dominating their field, there isn't room for another expert. Nothing could be further from the truth. In the cooking world, well-known experts include Martha Stewart, Paula Deen, and Emeril Lagasse. Did that stop Rachael Ray from making her mark?

The reality is that there are many experts for every subject, just as there are many books written for every genre. The key is to figure out what is unique or different about what you do as an expert and then find your audience.

Establishing expertise online is totally within your power. The first step is to claim your expert status. You can simply append it to your title or build your personal brand around your expertise.

For example, Joan Stewart is a self-proclaimed publicity expert. As a former news editor, Stewart teaches people how to generate publicity and capture media attention. She has taken this a step further by branding her business and her website as The Publicity Hound (publicityhound.com).

Several years ago, I decided it was time to call myself a small business expert. Do I know everything there is to know about running every small business under the sun? Absolutely not. Do I know more than most people? I believe I do. I stay on top of industry trends by reading relevant news, devouring books and studying business success stories. I have started several businesses and sold a business. I am fascinated by virtually every aspect of business and marketing, so much so that I list it as one of my hobbies. I teach classes on related subjects, write books, and conduct speaking engagements. That makes me an expert.

Incidentally, I publish this designation with everything that I do. Identifying myself as a small business expert has led to tremendous media opportunities and ultimately, more book sales.

Are there other small business experts out there? Absolutely. But I don't spend any time worrying about competition. Quite honestly, I would rather befriend them—we can find amazing ways to work together. I set myself apart by providing relevant, useful resources and information. Some may like my style, some may prefer my competitor's style. But there is room in the marketplace for each of us and we can thrive in our expert roles by being good at what we do.

The point here is that you are the expert at your subject matter. Whether through real-world experience, education or both, you have a unique understanding of your topic and can develop notoriety around that once you make the decision to own your expert status.

Experts and the Media

Take a look at any major magazine or newspaper article and you will see that experts are always cited. The same is true of news programs and comprehensive news stories. Media professionals are continually in need of experts to quote as sources because experts add credibility to the reporting.

Citations may be as simple as a quote of one or two lines:

Nurse Judy Johnson agrees. She notes that "Health care costs are on the rise..."

According to Adam Attorney, author of *The Lawyer's Guide to Small Business Taxes*, "Most businesses are missing out on opportunities to claim deductions..."

There is an entire chapter in this book devoted to getting media attention utilizing free and low-cost online resources. But if you want a quick way to get listed as an expert for media opportunities, there are some ways you can break out the pocketbook and pay to be at the media's disposal.

ProfNet.com is one of the leading sources that journalists and other media professionals use to locate experts. Though media professionals can search this massive database for free, experts must pay a substantial annual fee to be listed. Many PR firms hold memberships to this site in order to get their clients listed. Fees are steep and are targeted toward organizations, though individuals who are willing to pay can be listed.

Another option is the annual Yearbook of Experts which is published by ExpertClick.com. This is a printed guide, complemented by an online profile that many media professionals utilize for finding expert sources.

Author = Expert

Publishing a book is an instant credibility builder and is your official certification to claim your expert status.

If you're looking for some good news in the media/expert locator arena, there is a new trend in the journalism world. I happen to be a member of several freelance organizations and have recently learned that more and more journalists are simply turning to Amazon.com to find expert sources.

The benefit for journalists is that they can search by topic and then sort by date, allowing them to find the most current expert on a given subject. This proves that publishing a book is the quickest way to establish expert credibility and status.

Also, once a journalist locates a relevant book and its author, she must then locate contact information for the author. The next step is to turn to Google or another search engine to locate the author's website. So if you don't have a website, or your site isn't professional or otherwise hurts your credibility, you could be missing out on major media opportunities.

Online Opportunities for Experts

One of the quickest ways to become known as an expert online is to volunteer to be one. AllExperts.com one of the best kept secrets on the Web. Visitors search this site for advice on subjects ranging from computers, technology, and hypnosis to outdoor recreation, science, style, business, and religion.

Subjects are managed by volunteer experts who answer site visitors' questions. I have been a volunteer small business expert on this site for many years. Though you won't be compensated for your participation monetarily, there are several key advantages:

- ✓ You decide how many e-mail questions you are willing to accept and answer per day so you can manage your time commitment.
- ✓ Answers are archived online indefinitely so other site visitors can search and find your excellent responses.
- ✓ With each message that you post, you can include your brief bio and Web link. This is a high-traffic website so adding your link here can equate to excellent standing.
- ✓ You are instantly recognized as an expert in your subject and may even receive inquiries from the media.

✓ You have the opportunity to learn from the people who send you questions. I notice which questions are asked repeatedly and have found inspiration for writing articles and books as a result.

Other expert-type directories are popping up online every day. If this format appeals to you, search the Web and find some additional opportunities. Some may even pay you for your words of wisdom.

Publish Articles

Publishing articles is by far one of my favorite book marketing strategies. You can promote your book by writing articles for other people's websites and e-zines. In exchange, the site owner should include your brief author bio (fifty words or so) along with your website link. Even though you should not directly promote your book in an article, readers will visit your site if they like what you have to say about a related topic. Publishing articles also builds your credibility in your field and expands your exposure to a broad audience.

Here is my current bio for articles:

> Stephanie Chandler is a small business expert and the author of *From Entrepreneur to Infopreneur: Make Money with Books, E-Books and Information Products*. She is the founder of BusinessInfoGuide.com, a directory of resources for entrepreneurs and ProPublishingServices.com, a custom writing business specializing in electronic newsletters, information marketing, and sales copy for websites and brochures.

I manage to get two Web links in there so I can promote my books and my business at the same time. My bio changes frequently, but I keep it handy in a Word document so I can post it quickly when needed. It's helpful if you can use the same bio for articles, posting on online forums, etc. I have an expanded version of the above bio that I use for my online profiles on MySpace, Amazon, Yahoo, etc.

Generating Article Ideas

How-to articles are always popular and a good place to start. But you can also write top-ten type articles (i.e. 13 Ways to Eliminate Dust) or write interesting or funny essays.

Here are some examples:

✓ The author of a career coach-type book could write articles about job hunting, effective interview skills, negotiating salaries, or dressing for success.

✓ A financial author could write articles about retirement planning, investing in stocks, college funds or rental property.

✓ A children's book author could write articles for parents or about fun activities to do with kids.

✓ A science fiction author could write about recent scientific findings or other theories.

✓ A romance writer could write dating tips, top ten romantic date ideas or create a list of the most romantic songs.

Many websites operate on a limited budget and appreciate articles written by experts. You can offer to swap articles with website owners and co-promote each other, or simply submit your article for consideration. Most sites that accept articles will list their submission guidelines somewhere within the site.

The best way to decide who you want to write for is to look for websites and e-zines that reach your target audience. Check out related trade associations—these often have newsletters that need good content. You can also search the Internet for keywords related to your book topic and begin building a list of many sites where you can potentially get your articles published.

There are also numerous content sites that allow you to post articles that others can reprint in their e-zines. This is a great opportunity to showcase your writing skills with others and the best part is that it's *free*. Following are some of my favorite content sites:

✓ ideamarketers.com
✓ ezinearticles.com
✓ amazines.com

You can expect to generate plenty of website traffic from your article marketing efforts. And the more articles you publish, the more your traffic and fan base will grow.

Keep in mind that every time one of your articles is published, your website link is also listed. The bonus result is that your ranking with the search engines improves when you have lots of websites linking to you.

Search engine optimization expert Jim Tendick recommends changing your bio frequently and embedding links in keyword-rich text whenever possible. He also encourages writers to take an article and rewrite it in several different ways. This is a quick and easy way to generate additional content that can get picked up by different sources.

Tendick conducted a test with article marketing. He first established a pen name for the article using a name that when typed in to Google didn't produce any results. He then published the article on numerous article content directory sites (he usually pushes each article out to 100 sites). Just two days later, when he typed the fake pen name in to Google, more than 1500 results appeared.

Repurpose, Reuse, Recycle

Make sure you are reusing the articles that you submit to websites for publication. If you're not receiving payment and are submitting them for publicity purposes only, then offer your work as a "reprint." This way you can continue to publish the same article over and over again.

You may also want to submit articles to print publications. The major magazines at the checkout stands are difficult to break into and won't accept reprints; however, there are dozens of smaller publications that will gladly accept well-written articles.

Use the market guides such as *Writer's Market* to find a variety of smaller magazines. You can also surf the Web to find industry and trade publications. Here is an example how to format an e-mail submission for an article:

Article Submission
10 Ways to Beat the Holiday Blues
By Annie Author
Word Count: 756

<Insert Complete Article Text>

About the Author:
Annie Author is the author of *Blues Busters: A Guide to Emotional Well Being*. Visit her website at annieauthor.com and sign up for the newsletter with tips for managing your emotional health.

*You are welcome to reprint this article provided the author resource box is included. Thank you very much for your consideration.

Annie Author
555-555-5555
Annie@annieauthor.com

I personally maintain a list of my favorite online and print publications. Whenever I write a new article, I e-mail it out to each source on my list and also publish it on article content sites (ezinearticles.com, ideamarketers.com, etc.). This process has led to my articles appearing on hundreds of websites, magazines, newsletters and newspapers. Oh, and by the way, some publications will even pay you for the right to reprint your articles. I occasionally receive checks from publications that have policies to buy reprint rights. They aren't big money makers, but I consider it my bonus coffee fund in addition to all of the great exposure I get from getting my name—and website address—in print.

Over time you should see your articles spanning across the Web. Make sure to Google yourself periodically so you can see how your Internet presence is growing.

Most important, don't forget to publish your articles on your own website and e-zine. Having articles on your website gives your readers more to enjoy and gives the search engines more reasons to find you.

As I mentioned before, one of the most popular articles on BusinessInfoGuide.com is one that profiles the owners of a shoe store. Apparently, there's not be much competition for Internet users searching for information on opening a shoe store. Those readers in turn discover my site and all of the other great resources available for entrepreneurs. I know things are working well if they sign up for my e-zine and eventually buy my books.

 **Hot Tip**

Keep a journal of your article ideas. You may find you have so many ideas you can't possibly tackle them all at once. Commit them to paper so you won't forget about them. I keep a small spiral notebook on my desk where I can jot article ideas down as they come to me.

Update Your Signature

Your e-mail signature is an important billboard for you as an author and you can make it as long or as detailed as you want. You can include your contact information, website URL, book title, a brief description of your book, and any other details that you want people to know about you. Consider modifying your signature periodically to keep the content fresh and interesting.

If you're communicating with the public through e-mail, your signature is essential. You never know where your messages will be forwarded or whose eye you will catch. It's best to avoid inserting images. Unfortunately many e-mail systems will route your message straight to the trash can if it includes attachments.

Here's a look at my current e-mail signature:

Stephanie Chandler
Small Business Expert ~ Author ~ Speaker
BusinessInfoGuide.com
ProPublishingServices.com

P.S. Check out my new book.
"From Entrepreneur to Infopreneur" (John Wiley & Sons) businessinfoguide.com/infopreneur-book.htm

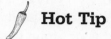 **Hot Tip**

Make sure you list http:// in front of your website URL anytime you post it online. For example:

Don't type it like this: www.BusinessInfoGuide.com

Instead type this: http://www.BusinessInfoGuide.com

While some e-mail providers and website pages will automatically activate a website link, many will leave the link static. This means that users will have to copy and paste the link in a browser in order to view the site. The http:// activates your link to make it clickable from most e-mail systems and Web pages.

Start an Online Group

Online groups can bring you tremendous exposure. Groups are essentially forums on the Internet that allow members to exchange messages about the group's primary subject matter. The benefit for you is similar to when you publish articles—you can include a signature that promotes your book and your website address. Often times the people who participate in groups do so on a regular basis, so over time you can become well known just for participating and soon you may have a whole new fan base.

You can start by joining one of the free groups hosted by Yahoo: groups.yahoo.com. To find a group that's right for you, search on keywords for your subject matter.

If you decide to start your own group, you will act as the moderator and can make decisions about who can join the group, the types of messages that are allowed, and whether or not you want members to be able to attach files or information to their posts. You can also send broadcast messages to group members. Visitors to Yahoo's group site can search keywords to locate active groups, which can bring a group owner new subscribers with very little effort.

Your group should have a niche focus that relates to your book. Keep in mind that you want your group to attract new readers, so make sure it appeals to your target audience.

Moderating a group can be time consuming so you need to be sure it's worth your effort. However, with enough promotion and word of mouth from new members, membership numbers have the potential to increase rapidly.

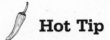 **Hot Tip**

Are you interested in starting or joining a local group and meeting in person? Check out Meetup.com to find groups in your city. You'll find every subject under the sun from religious and political groups to mom's clubs and business groups. There is a nominal fee to host a group, but the exposure can be tremendous. Each member also gets an online profile which can help you build exposure online, right in your own backyard.

Forums and Message Boards

Forums are similar to Yahoo groups because they encourage participation of visitors. The primary difference is that members do not necessarily have to subscribe and there can be numerous subtopics. Some service providers also allow you to run forums right inside your website.

Establishing your own forum or message board can attract visitors to your site through keyword searches. Hosting an active forum on your website can also encourage visitors to return frequently. If you are the author of a controversial topic or something people like to talk about, your forum could become quite popular.

Do keep in mind the amount of time involved in monitoring message boards as well as the possible legal implications. If you are concerned about the potential content you want to allow on your message board, be sure to seek the counsel of a lawyer before you begin.

You can also participate in other people's message boards. The value here is that when you post a message, you can include your signature and a link back to your website. The more you participate on a particular board, the more the other visitors will recognize your name.

To find message boards for your topic, conduct some Internet searches with keywords. If your topic is marketing, search for "marketing forum," "marketing message board," or "marketing discussion."

Forum Technology Providers

- ✓ PHPBB: phpbb.com
- ✓ World Crossing: http://wc0.worldcrossing.com
- ✓ BulletinBoards.com: bulletinboards.com
- ✓ Ryze.com: ryze.com
- ✓ Collective X: collectivex.com

Update Bio on All Membership Directories

This is an easy task to overlook. Take an inventory of all the organizations and websites where you are a member or have a profile listed and visit all of them. Update your profile to indicate that you are the author of *XYZ* book and include your website link. Don't forget sites like Yahoo! and Amazon.com—anywhere that you have updated personal information that is publicly available.

To make this process easy, write a short and long version of your bio and save the file to a place on your computer that you can easily access. This makes it easy for you to copy and paste your information to any new profile that you create and also ensures that your bio is consistent on all sites where you are listed.

Public Speaking

Public speaking is one of the best and most traditional ways to build an audience for your book. Speaking to a group or teaching classes on a related subject has many advantages:

✓ You are instantly perceived as an expert.
✓ You have the best opportunity to sell yourself and your book by giving a compelling presentation and creating immediate fans.
✓ The group that hosts you will provide you with free promotion by announcing your appearance to their mailing list or in their catalog.
✓ You can sell your books and other products at the back of the room (make sure you will be allowed to do this, otherwise it's probably not worth your time).

Not everyone is a fan of public speaking but with a little practice, you can be an expert at it in no time. Practice also helps reduce the fear of speaking. If you're nervous about taking this on, consider joining a local Toastmasters group (toastmasters.org). These groups help develop professional speakers and build confidence.

There are also plenty of speaker coaching classes and schools. Several years ago I attended a week-long speaking course. We were forced to give short speeches that were recorded on video, and then we went back in a room to review the video with a coach.

After getting over the agony of having to watch myself on film, I quickly learned to refine my skills. There would be no more jingling of change in my pocket, fiddling with a pen in my hands or stepping nervously from side to side. Those things look really awful on video.

Below are a few more tips for effective speaking engagements.

Prepare, Prepare, Prepare

Do your best to memorize your entire presentation and if nothing else, at least memorize your opening lines. If you get up to the microphone and can't even remember your first line, it's going to be a long and painful talk for everyone. But if you can at least get your speech started, you can go into autopilot for the rest of the talk.

Write a Great Presentation

The industry standard for PowerPoint slides is one slide for every two to three minutes. So if you're giving a thirty-minute presentation, you should have just ten to fifteen slides. Anything more and you will likely go over in time—something the event organizers and attendees won't appreciate.

PowerPoint 101

If you do decide to use slides (I personally try to avoid them), take advantage of your skills as a writer and follow the old rule of "show, don't tell." Ideally your slides should visually enhance your presentation by demonstrating ideas with images. Slides that are bogged down by text are boring. Worse yet, it can be tempting to read from your slides. To keep the audience awake and happy, use plenty of images or avoid using slides altogether.

Pace Yourself

If you tend to talk too fast or you are extremely nervous, take slow, deep breaths between sentences. This forces you to pause, and though it may seem like a long and painful pause to you, it actually gives your audience a chance to absorb what you just said.

Practice Pays Off

As crazy as it may sound, practice your speech in an empty room. The more you rehearse, the more polished you will sound. If you're really brave, get out the video recorder and watch yourself. I promise that you will quickly break a few bad habits.

Warm Up the Audience

Many speakers try to open with humor. True, it can be a great ice breaker, but if it's not your style, you still have options. You can open by complimenting the city that you're in, the conference you are attending or the audience in general. Compliments almost always make good ice breakers, especially when they are genuine.

Watch the Time

Ask someone in the audience to give you a signal when you have ten or five minutes left. This will give you a chance to wrap up.

Develop a Killer Closing

If you want the audience to remember you, then do or say something memorable. Think of a powerful way to drive your message home. You can do a funny dance, give something away, read a quote or short story, or espouse some fantastic words of wisdom. Whatever you do, put your unique signature on your presentation and end with a bang.

Ask for the Sale

Nothing is worse than giving a great presentation and then forgetting to ask for the sale. I have been guilty of this myself. When concluding your presentation, you can simply say something like, "I'll be at my autograph table in the back for the next few minutes if you would like to get a copy of my book." It's a soft sell and it works.

Venues for Speaking Engagements

Once you have decided to venture into speaking to promote your books, you should find plenty of possibilities. Start in the area where you live and in major surrounding cities. Once you have mastered speaking locally, you will be ready to expand your reach.

Consider the following possibilities for conducting speaking engagements or teaching classes.

✓ Trade associations—These often have monthly meetings and are always in need of speakers. Consider associations in and outside of your topic specialty. For example, the author of an investment advice guide can target mom's groups, human resources associations, business groups, the chamber of commerce, real estate investment clubs, etc.

✓ Adult learning centers—I teach at the Learning Annex in San Francisco and the Learning Exchange in Sacramento. The exposure I get from just being in these catalogs is phenomenal.

✓ Schools—From grade schools to colleges, all schools host a variety of events and programs featuring speakers.

✓ Colleges—For quick notoriety and credibility, consider teaching a related class at nearby colleges.

✓ Local bookstores—Instead of holding a boring book signing event, host a discussion. These are far more likely to attract an audience as well as media attention. Also, children's book authors are always in demand for readings.

✓ Industry-related businesses—Depending on the nature of your book's topic, contact businesses that would be interested in an informative presentation for their employees.

Resources for Professional Speaking

✓ SpeakerNetNews: speakernetnews.com
✓ Speaker Match: speakermatch.com
✓ BusinessInfoGuide: businessinfoguide.com/speaking.htm
✓ Learning Annex: learningannex.com
✓ Toastmasters: toastmasters.com
✓ National Speakers Association: nsaspeaker.org
✓ Professional Speakers Association: professional-speakers.org
✓ The Jokes: the-jokes.com
✓ Jokes: jokes.com
✓ Famous Quotes: quotationspage.com
✓ *Speak and Grow Rich* by Dottie Walters and Lilly Walters

Author Interview

Author: Hal Elrod

Book: *Taking Life Head On (The Hal Elrod Story)*

website: yopalhal.com

What is your book about?

Taking Life Head On is the unbelievable true story of Hal Elrod's inspiring life, after death. At age twenty, Hal was struck head on by a drunk driver and found dead at the scene. Six days later he woke from a coma to the devastating news that he had suffered thirteen broken bones, permanent brain damage, and that he might never walk again. Defying the logic of doctors and the temptations to be a victim, he found strength through the powers of faith, love, gratitude, and responsibility, and he bounced back.

What led you to publish the book?

I was overwhelmed with a gratitude for my life and a sense of responsibility to help others through the power of my story.

How has being an author changed or improved your life personally or professionally?

Being an author has improved my life in a multitude of ways, both personally and professionally. Personally, it was one of the most challenging tasks I've ever taken on, thus giving me a sense of humility as well as pride, and the confidence in myself that I can take on such a challenge again. Professionally, it has given me more credibility than I ever expected, as well as resulting in a steady influx of paying coaching clients and paid speaking engagements.

What online marketing methods have worked best for you?

I have found some success utilizing social networking sites, such as MySpace, but the majority of my results have come through e-mail marketing to my own mailing list.

Are there any methods you have used that haven't yielded impressive results?

Not really, I typically only model others' and use methods that have proven successful.

Do you have a favorite off-line book marketing strategy?

My favorite off-line book marketing strategy has been and remains selling books to the audience after my speeches, although this is something I resisted doing for the first year after I published my book. During my speech I am able to establish my expertise and plant seeds for my book, then back-of-the-room sales are a natural progression.

Do you own a business?

I cofounded *Global Empowerment Coaching* with my good friend and business partner, Jon Berghoff. We offer three services: coaching, consulting, and keynote speaking. We provide strategic systems for improving performance to sales people, entrepreneurs, managers, and business owners.

How do you view the advantages or disadvantages of self-publishing vs. traditional publishing?

The main advantage I see with self-publishing is the ability to generate a much higher profit for every book that you sell. My research led me to the conclusion that most traditional publishers pay pennies on the dollar to their authors. So, it is important to be clear as to your purpose in publishing your work: If it is to make money, self-publish; if it is to gain exposure and establish credibility, you may want to consider gaining the marketing horsepower of a traditional publisher behind you. (Although be aware that most traditional/major publishers—who may be publishing anywhere from ten to fifty or more books per week—allocate very little marketing dollars and efforts to the majority of their authors.)

What advice do you have for other authors?

I have two pieces of advice for other authors:

1. Make an unwavering *commitment* to working on your book until it is finished, no matter what it takes or how difficult it may become at times. Decide ahead of time (and be okay with the fact) that you will likely face obstacles such as self-doubt, frustration, writer's block, fear of failure, perfectionism, disgust for your work, hopelessness, complacency, and just plain boredom—to name a few—but that it is okay to feel those things and follow through with your commitment to write anyway. If you have value to give, if your story/knowledge/ideas will make a positive impact in the lives of your readers, then you must take on a deep feeling of responsibility to share your value with the world. Having an attitude of "it's not about me" during these difficult times allowed me to push through them and keep working, because I felt that doing so was truly my dutiful contribution to the world.

2. Set up a system of *accountability* to keep you on track. You can do this through written time lines, hiring a coach, or simply setting up some agreements with friends or family members who will remain committed to your progress and completion.

CHAPTER 6

Online Marketing Strategies

This chapter is really the core of this entire book. We are here to talk about how to leverage the Internet to sell more books—and we do that by marketing online. The opportunities are endless and new opportunities are introduced every day as the World Wide Web continues to evolve. I can't imagine how hard it must have been to promote books just twenty or thirty years ago.

As you have probably noticed from reading the author profiles in this book, there are some themes in the methods most have used to generate publicity. This chapter covers some of the most popular strategies for building your online presence. And like most of the topics covered in this book, these methods require minimum investment and can generate maximum return.

If you want to truly be successful as an author, you really have no choice but to embrace marketing. But once you do, it can make it all worthwhile.

Send a Newsletter/E-zine

No matter what kind of book you are promoting, an electronic newsletter (also known as an e-zine) is essential. A newsletter provides the opportunity to create ongoing communications with your fans and prospective readers. You can also use it to advertise new books, products, services, or events. Your site visitors will appreciate the effort and can become fans for life simply because you publish an interesting newsletter.

If you want to boost subscribers to your e-zine, give people some incentive to sign up. You might offer a free sample chapter from your book or a related special report as a bonus. I currently offer the report "10 Ways to Generate Multiple Streams of Income" to visitors who sign up on BusinessInfoGuide.com and it works like a charm.

Give readers a reason to read and keep your e-zine by including a special coupon, recipe or useful article. You can even turn your e-zine into a new revenue stream by selling advertising space to businesses.

Sending e-zines through e-mail is inexpensive and easy to do. An e-mail based newsletter does not need to be flashy. It's more important that it is easy to read and the content is valuable. Using graphics can make it difficult for some readers to open or even receive your message if they don't have high speed Internet access, so minimize the use of graphic images.

Here are some ideas for inclusion in your newsletter:

✓ Brief letter to your customers (this is essential and helps them feel like they know you)
✓ Calendar of events, book signing tour schedule, or classes you are teaching
✓ New book announcement
✓ Promotion or sale information (special offers generate sales.)
✓ A coupon
✓ A recipe
✓ Articles on subjects related to your book(s)
✓ Recommended resources (related Web links, software, etc.)
✓ Book review (of someone else's book)
✓ Question and answer column
✓ Reviews from readers
✓ Case studies or reader success stories
✓ Advertisements for businesses
✓ Community information
✓ Articles submitted by readers
✓ Quick tips (typically a few sentences about something useful)

✓ Resources (website URLs, phone numbers, addresses, etc.)
✓ Frequently asked questions
✓ Contest announcements
✓ Famous quotes
✓ Comic strips
✓ Crossword puzzles or similar games
✓ Top ten-type lists ("10 Ways to Motivate Employees," "12 Reasons to Refinance Your Business Loan," etc.)
✓ Masthead (list of contributors)
✓ Industry-related statistics
✓ Industry news
✓ Column written by a contributor
✓ Photos
✓ Results of a reader survey
✓ Letters to the editor/feedback from readers
✓ Product reviews
✓ Graphs, tables or charts
✓ General announcements
✓ Classified ads
✓ Birthdays or anniversaries
✓ Historical events/dates
✓ Poem
✓ Excerpt from a book
✓ Excerpt from a blog
✓ Recommendations (music, products, services, etc.)

If you don't want to write all of the content yourself, you can access free articles on a variety of topics from websites like IdeaMarketers.com, ezinearticles.com, and Amazines.com. You could also have your readers contribute some of the content. Ask them to submit articles, tips, feedback, and other useful information. Also consider summarizing entries from your blog.

Don't be afraid to promote your books within your newsletter. As long as you are providing plenty of useful and interesting free content, readers will be glad to know about the opportunity to purchase your work.

Tips for Newsletter Success:

Encourage new subscribers by making it easy to sign up from every page on your website.

Figure out what your subscribers want to know and earn their loyalty by delivering valuable content.

Never send unsolicited e-mail. Spammers are running rampant in cyberspace and the quickest way to lose fans is to send unsolicited messages. Make sure you have a privacy policy and stick to it.

Beware of spam filters. The algorithms are changing so fast that it's nearly impossible to keep up, but there are certain words that can stop your messages from getting through. Avoid using words like *Free*, *Sex*, and *Money*.

Be consistent with delivery. If you promise a weekly e-zine, send it out on the same day each week. Sending it monthly is fine too and probably appropriate for most authors.

Insert a note encouraging subscribers to "Share this newsletter with a friend."

To comply with current CAN Spam Act regulations, you should include a link or instructions for customers to unsubscribe to your newsletter. You shouldn't receive many unsubscribe requests if your content is perceived as valuable.

Remember to include your contact information and website URL in all of your correspondence with readers.

Service Providers

Sending a newsletter via e-mail becomes challenging as your list grows larger. If you are using an e-mail program such as Microsoft Outlook or AOL mail, the system may choke when you attempt to send too many messages at once. Spam filters on the recipient's end may also block a large broadcast from being received.

Once your list exceeds fifty or so subscribers, you should consider investing in a newsletter management system. There are numerous providers to choose from and the fees range from $10 to $100 or more per month depending on the number of subscribers you manage and how many broadcasts you send. These systems allow you to send out mass mailings and create forms on your website that make it easy for new subscribers to join.

Some providers also offer templates for newsletter design and the ability to set up auto responders. Auto responders are used to automate your responses to e-mail or proactively send messages to people on your list.

Automating your e-mail management frees up your time to focus on your business and gives you a professional edge over competitors who are attempting to do it all manually.

Electronic Newsletter Technology Providers:

✓ Constant Contact: constantcontact.com
✓ 1Shopping Cart: 1shoppingcart.com
✓ Zinester: zinester.com

Social Networking

When MySpace.com came out of the woodwork, I was convinced it was just the latest hot fad for teenagers. I have since changed my tune. As it turns out, it's also a popular destination for authors, business owners, artists and millions of people looking to make new connections.

It's free to set up your profile with information about you. You can upload a photo, list details about your books, and begin connecting with people in the community. There are many other ways to leverage MySpace. From blogs and videos to events calendars and chat rooms, there are seemingly endless possibilities for finding your target audience here.

Social networking doesn't stop with MySpace, it is only just beginning. I only recently set up an account on LinkedIn and have a lot of fun connecting with old friends. Remember, it's all about your sphere of influence. Even finding friends from grade school or past careers can help you build exposure for your books. Most people love to tell their friends and family about their author-friend's books.

Here are some places where you can set up a profile and start connecting online:

- ✓ LinkedIn.com—Primarily for connecting with professional relationships (people you worked with, went to school with, etc.)
- ✓ Facebook.com—Focused on connecting with friends and people with related interests
- ✓ Friendster.com—The name says it all—connect with friends. Only meant for use by adults (must be 18 years old to participate)
- ✓ eCademy.com—Mostly business-related
- ✓ Spoke.com—Business and sales focus
- ✓ Tickle.com—Features categories including lifestyle, mind & body, relationship, style & beauty, entertainment and more
- ✓ Tribe.com—Based on the city where you live, you can become active in your community—online

If you want to take social networking to a new level, consider starting your own social networking site. You can set up your own site with whatever niche topic you choose. Check out ning.com.

Virtual Book Tours

Would you like to promote your book in your underwear? While you would likely draw a crowd if you showed up at your local bookstore in your skivvies, I am not advocating indecent exposure. An even better idea is to host a virtual book tour.

Typically virtual book tours are conducted by having the author make guest appearances in Internet chat rooms, message boards and blogs. But these tours are limited only by your imagination. They can also include Internet radio interviews and podcasts, videos, telesminars, webcasts, and more.

Book tours are conducted during a specified time frame in order to maximize the sense of urgency. Tours range from a few days to a few weeks, though you may only need to commit a few hours each day to the actual tour.

For example, Jane Author might host her virtual book tour from October 1 through the 14. During those two weeks, she would fill her calendar with as many online promotion opportunities as possible. She might conduct an Internet radio interview on Monday morning, post a guest blog entry on Monday afternoon, be a guest on a live Internet chat on Tuesday morning, post an article on another blog that afternoon, and so on.

Be prepared to send out several complimentary copies of your book. Anyone who commits to interview you will likely want a review copy of your book first. Be sure to start scheduling your tour at least six weeks prior to the commencement date. You will want to give yourself enough time to schedule your appearances and send out copies of your book.

Following are steps for setting up your own virtual book tour. You may want to consider getting some help from someone who can help find connections for you. While you can certainly spend time searching for appropriate markets for your tour, you can accelerate the process by leveraging the services of a virtual assistant or someone who has experience with this type of promotion.

Virtual Book Tour Plan

1. Write up an interesting book tour announcement that you can e-mail to potential tour stops. Include a brief overview of your book along with your author bio. It will also help your cause if you can offer something in return (a mutually beneficial offer is always better than simply asking for someone to give you something). You can offer to promote the blog or chat room that will be hosting you by listing them on your website, blog and/or in your newsletter. If you want to up the ante, offer to give away a copy of your book or other prize to the audience.

2. Create a page on your website with your book overview, author bio, and book tour dates. Don't forget

a promotional photo that people can download if needed. An excerpt or sample chapter is also a good addition. You can send this link along with your pitch to potential tour candidates.

3. Leverage your strategic alliances. Contact people in your network or circle of influence and ask if they can recommend any venues for your book tour. Better yet, ask them to make an introduction or recommendation for you.

4. Start compiling a list of potential tour stops. Search the Internet for related blogs, chat rooms, websites, Internet radio shows and any other venue that reaches your target reading audience.

5. Once you have a few tour stops scheduled, publish your calendar on your website. Begin building buzz as early as possible.

6. Develop an extensive list of interview questions. Your hosts will likely ask for these and will be grateful that you have them ready.

7. Write some brief articles related to your book and have them ready for requesters.

8. Send a reminder to each host of your tour stop twenty-four hours before your appearance. Though the event will be engraved on your calendar, it could have slipped through the cracks for your host.

9. Write posts about your virtual book tour experience on your blog following each appearance. If you don't have a blog, start one. This is a great place to get exposure and build momentum for your tour. This is also a great way to thank your hosts since you can post links back to their blogs and related sites.

10. Don't forget to send a thank you note to everyone who invites you to stop by during your tour. This will help them remember you in the future. You never know where strategic alliances might be formed. Plus, it's just a nice thing to do.

Sample Tour E-mail Inquiry:

Dear <insert name here—make it personal.>,

My name is Willie Writer and I am the author of "The Complete Guide to Spiders." I discovered your excellent blog/chatroom/Internet radio show recently and thoroughly enjoyed your post about XYZ [compliments never hurt and a comment like this also shows that you took the time to view their site].

I am getting ready to launch my new book and would like to invite you to participate in my virtual book tour. In exchange, I will help promote your blog/chat room/Internet radio show on my website and in my e-zine. You will also have the opportunity to earn commission on any book sales that you make.

Here's the scoop: Between February 1 and February 10, I will be making various virtual stops at venues across the Internet including blogs, chat rooms, and Internet radio shows. I am flexible about how each book tour stop will work and can offer you any of the following:

✓ An advance copy of my book for your review
✓ A scheduled interview over the phone
✓ A chat room interview
✓ An article written especially for your audience
✓ An affiliate link so that you can earn commission on any resulting book sales

I believe you have a perfect audience for my book and I promise to be a fun and engaging guest. Are you interested? I would love to discuss this further with you.

Warm regards,
Willie

P.S. Below is an overview of my book and my author bio. Additional details are also available on my website at www...

Resources for Book Tour Promotion:

✓ Book Place allows members to share and promote their books: morganmandelbooks.ning.com
✓ John Kremer's Book Marketing Network is another valuable resource for authors: bookmarket.ning.com
✓ The Writer's Life group on Yahoo! encourages authors to self-promote: groups.yahoo.com/group/thewriterslife
✓ The Beyond the Books blog is specifically dedicated to interviewing authors on virtual book tours (various fiction genres): beyondthebooks.authorsabode.com

Teleseminars

Teleseminars, also known as teleclasses, are conducted via conference call. Participants dial-in to a conference line to listen, and the host either conducts a talk or more commonly, interviews a guest.

I have personally been a guest on dozens of teleseminars and have found them to be excellent venues for book sales. The host typically has a substantial e-mail list and will promote the teleseminar to the list several times before the actual event. Whether the host decides to sell my book or simply mentions it during the promotion and the call itself, I always see book sales spike as a result.

The best teleseminars are instructional and offer how-to information to listeners. Some authors charge an admission fee for their teleseminars (from $10 to $30), while others offer them for free. Either way, these events can be recorded and made available for download (again for free or for a fee).

Michelle Ulrich, a business and Internet marketing strategist whose company exclusively works with authors and speakers (MichelleUlrich.com), recommends hosting your own events for free. "If you are not well known, have a small e-mail list (or no list) and want to grow your list, it is suggested to host no-cost teleseminars for about a year (or less) packed with incredible content and interesting topics. After you gain a fan base, start paid teleseminars on topics you know really well."

Promoting your teleseminars to events calendars and other online venues is a great way to boost attendance, according to

Ulrich. She adds, "Not only does this increase exposure for your event, but it increases your exposure overall. If someone notices your teleseminar topic and finds it interesting, they are more likely to check out your website, books, etc."

Ulrich recommends posting your events on the following websites:

- ✓ MySpace.com
- ✓ FastPitchNetworking.com—Sign up for the $14.95 per month package to announce your own events and teleclasses
- ✓ xing.com—A global market for your events and teleclasses and there's no need to sign up for the monthly fee-based membership
- ✓ Craigslist.org—List in your city or a nearby major metropolitan area
- ✓ fullcalendar.com—Again, list in your city or a nearby major metropolitan area; it's highly worth the $19.95 for the exposure

Teleseminars will probably work best for nonfiction authors, though I'm sure there are some creative fiction authors out there who can find a way to leverage this promotion opportunity.

If you don't yet have an audience large enough to support your own teleseminars, it's worthwhile to contact others who are hosting these and offer to be a guest. Of course, the bigger the audience, the better, but even if you only end up with fifteen people on your call, you've likely been promoted to a much wider group.

An alternative to the teleseminar is a webinar, which is a combination of a conference call and a Web-based presentation. Attendees to webinars can watch the action on their screen which makes webinars useful for those who want to provide an instructional demonstration on the computer or complement a presentation with PowerPoint slides.

Before you forge ahead with teleseminars, be sure to attend some other people's teleseminars to get a firsthand idea of what they're all about. The best teleseminars are primarily informational and aren't heavy on a sales pitch. Unfortunately there are many online marketers out there offering free "informational" teleseminars as a ploy to get listeners to listen to their sales pitch. Do me a favor and don't emulate these people. They are ruining the value of these events for the rest of us.

There are scores of service providers out there who offer the conference call functionality required to host teleseminars. Rates are also constantly changing. The best way to find a provider is to perform an Internet search and then carefully compare current price and options. For example, some will give you a dial-in number for free, but will charge you if you want to offer toll-free access. Some charge per person who attends the teleseminar; some may include recording services for free while others make this an add-on. This industry is getting more competitive by the day so do your homework and shop around for the best price and service.

Tips Sheets & Booklets

Tips sheets can be a fantastic marketing tool. Assemble a list of helpful tips that are of interest to your target audience and you can give them away, sell them or use them as bonus items. Your tips could be as few as ten or as many as 100.

I publish tips everywhere. The back of my business card has "Benefits of an Electronic Newsletter." I frequently conduct speaking engagements and hand out a list of "My Favorite Online Resources."

I also have a printed booklet called "35 Ways to Tune-Up Your Website and Boost Revenues Online." I hand this out at speaking engagements and trade shows to promote Pro Publishing Services, my electronic newsletter and writing business. Just recently I received a call from someone who attended one of my speaking engagements where I handed out these booklets. The caller requested several dozen copies to give away to her business network group. I didn't hesitate to drop them in the mail because this equates to free publicity.

Here are some additional examples:

✓ A financial advisor could assemble a tips sheet called "20 Ways to Save on Tax Planning."

✓ A science fiction author could offer something fun like "12 Ways to Meet an Alien."

✓ A beauty book author could offer "10 Tips for Ageless Skin."

✓ A parenting author could give away "25 Tips for Child Safety."

✓ A travel author could provide "10 Ways to Save on Your Next Vacation."

Offer your tips for free as a bonus for registering for your e-zine or buying one of your books. If your website is set up with auto responders, you can automate the entire delivery process.

Another way to use tips sheets is to offer them to other authors and businesses to give away. When another website leverages your tips as a promotional item, you get exposure to potential new readers.

By offering something of real value, people will be more likely to hang on to your list and refer to it over and over again, thus providing a consistent reminder of your book, business or web-site. Make sure your contact information is included and that you strike an agreement to include your contact information with any-one who reproduces your tips.

You can also submit your tips to websites and e-zines just as you do your articles. Quick tips make great fillers for all kinds of publications.

Lastly, these make great handouts at book signing events and speaking engagements. Even if the reader doesn't buy your book, the free tips sheet or booklet could eventually lead to a book sale or to the reader signing up for your e-zine and eventually buying your book. Some take longer than others. Giving away something tangible and interesting gives recipients a reason to remember you later. I have also seen authors print tips on bookmarks—a great way to stand out.

Strategic Alliances

Your books can reach Australia, England, Japan, and back if you want them to. The first step is to get in touch with other authors and website owners across the Internet and see how you can work together.

The key to successful alliances is to offer something that is beneficial to both parties. You also want to make sure you are partnering with people who reach your target audience. In some cases, you may even want to partner with your competition. You know the old saying, "Keep your friends close and your enemies closer"? When you stop viewing your competition as the enemy, you could uncover some great ways you can complement each other. Here are some ideas:

✓ Swap links to each other's websites.

✓ Trade advertising space on each other's Web pages.

✓ Trade advertising space in each other's e-zines.

✓ Publish each other's articles in e-zines.

✓ Publish excerpts of each other's books.

✓ Give away each other's tips sheets or e-books as bonuses with product purchases.

✓ Support each other with new book releases. Though your time lines may be different, make sure each is committed to helping with announcements when a new release date approaches.

✓ Offer an affiliate program to make it financially worthwhile for others to promote your books. If your shopping cart system doesn't provide it, check out PayDotCom.com or PayLoadz.com for free affiliate accounts.

✓ Cohost a teleseminar.

Make sure to personalize your initial contact with the author or website owner. Send a thoughtful e-mail or pick up the phone and call. Introduce yourself and give a genuine compliment about the person's book or website. Suggest ways that you can help him. Then wait and let him offer up some ways to help you.

If he has a mailing list of 10,000, and you only have 1,000, offer to run his ad for six months vs. the one or three months that he runs yours. If he likes you, he may not even care that you're on different levels of the playing field.

To locate strategic alliance partners, start by searching the Internet for keywords that are complimentary to your subject matter. For example, if you are the author of a book about travel, you could search for hotels, tour companies, catering companies, and travel agents. Notice the sites that are listed in the top twenty—those are likely getting the most traffic for your industry.

Once you locate potential partners, start contacting them one by one. You don't have to do this all in one day. In fact, it may be beneficial to start slowly so you can see what kind of response you get when you try different methods. If your methods aren't working, evaluate and modify your pitch until you see results. Over time you should be able to build up a solid list of key relationships.

As with any business contact or friend, be sure to nurture the relationship. Check in periodically or share an interesting article or piece of news of interest to your strategic partner. Send kudos when you see his name mentioned in the media or let him know when you've seen his ad somewhere. When you treat strategic relationships with the same respect you treat your friends, you build loyalty that can last a lifetime.

Accidental Alliances

When I was getting ready to release my first book, I sent press releases out to all of the major business magazines. Apparently they actually do read these releases because an editor at *Entrepreneur Magazine* forwarded mine to one of their writers, Romanus Wolter.

The title of my new book was going to be *The Business Startup Checklist and Planning Guide: Kick Start Your Entrepreneurial Dreams!* I performed careful research to make sure that my title was unlike any other book title out there—but it never occurred to me to check the subtitle.

Can you tell what is coming next?

Romanus sent me a pleasant e-mail pointing out that my subtitle was a bit close to his book's main title: *Kick Start Your Dream Business*. I was mortified. Fortunately the book still had a few days before going to press and the publisher was able to make last minute changes before it was too late. I simply took out "Kick Start" and replaced it with "Seize Your Entrepreneurial Dreams!"

Romanus and I ended up exchanging several e-mail messages and before I knew it, we were fast friends. We ended up working together on several projects, including teleseminars and speaking engagements. We also promoted each other in our respective e-zines and still forward each other occasional leads for publicity opportunities.

The point is that you never know where your alliances might come from. It so happens that Romanus and I could be seen as rivals since we both target a similar audience, but neither of us ever looked at it that way. When you put the interest of others first, somehow that good karma comes back around.

Try This:

Make a list of the people you already know who would make good strategic alliance partners. Also list ideas for how you can work together (swap advertising in e-zines, promote each other's products, cohost seminars, etc.). Remember, it's best to lead with a description of how *you* can help your partner. If your partner doesn't return the favor by offering to help you, then it's time to ask for what you want.

Hold a Contest

People love to get stuff for free and contests are a great way to attract new visitors to your website and, ultimately, new readers for your book.

Here are some contest ideas:

✓ Have kids submit stories related to your book's theme.
✓ Have readers submit funny slogans.
✓ Hold a poetry contest with a theme related to your book.
✓ Have people submit their best solutions to problems related to your book. For example, if you wrote a gardening manual, readers could submit their best gardening tips. Take this a step further and publish the entries in a booklet when the contest is over.
✓ Host a recipe contest if you have a cooking-related book.

Get creative and have fun with your contest ideas. I've seen website owners host contests as a way of gathering testimonials, and others have given away consulting services as an award for the best story submission. Gift cards or electronic downloads (e-books) are also great incentives. Find something that creates a buzz so you can reel in new traffic and exposure for your books.

Be sure to promote your contest not only on your website and in your e-zine, but on other people's websites. Ask alliance partners to make announcements for you and submit your contest to online message boards. A contest is also a newsworthy reason to send a press release.

 **Hot Tip**

Ask other authors to contribute their books as prizes. They will want to do so in order to get the added exposure. Then you can in turn offer your book to them and create a strategic alliance.

Start an Affiliate Program

An affiliate program is a way to offer incentive to others to help sell your books by paying a commission for each sale. In most cases, you can offer a percentage or flat dollar amount for each sale generated by your affiliates.

The major online shopping cart services provide an option to create your own affiliate program. Some other affiliate services to consider are Clickbank.com and PayDotCom.com.

If you do offer affiliate sales, you want to make it as easy as possible for your affiliates to be successful. Offer complete descriptions of your books and high-quality images that your affiliates can use on their websites. You might even want to host a teleseminar to teach your affiliates how to best make money by selling your books.

You can also encourage others to sell through Amazon's Associates program. The benefit here is that Amazon handles everything and pays the commission directly so you don't have to worry about tracking payments. All you need to do is sit back and watch your sales numbers soar. See the chapter on success with Amazon for more details.

Additional Strategies

Get Testimonials

Whenever anyone says something nice about your book, use it to your advantage. Print testimonials on all marketing materials and on your website. To obtain testimonials, just ask. Contact your readers via your e-zine and ask them to write a paragraph about your book. Or if you receive fan mail (and you should if your online marketing strategies are working), ask if you can reprint the writer's comments. Be sure to get permission to reprint from anyone who provides you with a testimonial.

Pre-Announce New Books

It's never too early to start building excitement around a new book. When your next book is in the works, it is perfectly acceptable to begin mentioning it on your website and in your e-zine several months before it is available. In fact, you should set up a pre-order system to solicit orders prior to the book release. If you do this, make sure you set a safe release date that you know you won't miss.

I started promoting my first book early and began receiving orders a full two months before the release date. If you have built a good audience of fans, they will be eager to support your new work.

Contact all Sources Referenced in Your Book

If your book mentions any companies, business owners, authors or websites, get in touch with those mentioned. Let them know you have given them some free publicity in your book. You can ask if they would be interested in reselling the book or offering a link to it from their website. Think strategically. How could your book benefit that business? Make your pitch.

Utilize Your Business

If you run a business in a field related to your book, maximize the opportunity to promote your book with your customers and business associates. You can provide details about your book on your website, in newsletters to customers, and even at your physical place of business. Look for ways to use your business to sell your book and start generating some buzz early in the process. You can also give your books away to clients and potential business partners.

I know an attorney who wrote a parenting book. Upon the release, she sent copies to all of the local family therapists. Her business quickly took off from that point forward.

How can your business benefit from your book? Or how can your book benefit from your business?

$$\overset{\frown}{\underset{\smile}{\fbox{Author Interview}}}$$

Author: Michelle Dunn

Most recent book: *The Ultimate Credit & Collections Handbook*

Total # of books published: Seven

Websites: michelledunn.com and credit-and-collections.com

What is your book about?

The Ultimate Credit and Collections Handbook helps businesses get their customers to pay them in full and on time. This book helps businesses make more money, without making a single extra sale, by collecting from their current customers more effectively. Weeding out bad accounts and offering credit only to qualified customers, resulting in more paid sales, increasing your cash flow with a streamlined, organized credit department, and navigating the confusing federal and state laws that govern debt collection will also help businesses get results.

What led you to publish the book?

I was a bill collector for eighteen years, and started and ran my own collection agency for eight years. I have written and implemented many credit policies for many different types of businesses. I have written seven books about debt collection and am the president of Credit & Collections Association with thousands of members.

When I owned my collection agency, most business owners I dealt with did not have any credit policy, and would place accounts with my agency over and over, losing money again and again. My books help business owners know what to do in order to stop that nonpayment cycle and make more money with less hassle.

How has being an author changed or improved your life personally or professionally?

Being an author changed my life within my industry because once the first book was published, most considered me an expert in my field. This leads to more questions from people, more book sales, more press, and more money.

What online marketing methods have worked best for you?

Writing articles and press releases and being consistent in sending them out to targeted media. The key is to make the releases or articles not about my book, but about my area of expertise and based on what is going on in the news. Ask yourself what people want to know about right now. Then write an article using that topic and incorporate your book's subject into it.

Are there any methods you have used that haven't yielded impressive results?

Placing classified ads in the *New York Times* only yielded crazy people contacting me.

Do you have a favorite off-line book marketing strategy?

I do a lot of direct mailings and include special offers and coupons. I write out a plan and follow it, which works much better than just trying to remember everything and trying to wing it.

Do you own a business?

I own my ten-year-old Credit & Collections Association that I started when I started my collection agency. This association helps to promote the importance, interest and education of a healthy credit environment in our society. I started it in 1998 and Credit & Collections has been providing thousands of members with information relative to the credit and debt collection industry for many years.

Has being an author helped your business in any way?

When I wrote my first book, *Starting a Collection Agency*, I used it as a marketing tool for my agency. In every example in the book I used my company information so it was everywhere. I promoted my Credit & Collections Association in the book and gained many new members that way. Also, once you write a book, you are perceived as an expert and gain credibility in your industry. I also had a very successful agency because I did a good job, so all of those things combined really boosted my business.

What advice do you have for other authors?

Write a marketing plan and *follow it*.
Do something to market yourself every day.
Don't give up.

CHAPTER 7

Online Media Opportunities

One of your priorities should be to get media attention for your book. It is the most inexpensive form of promotion, as well as one of the most powerful. When the media hypes a book, people listen and may be more inclined to accept the recommendation even more than if it came from a friend.

You will use your media list to send press releases and pitch story ideas. Your goal should be to ultimately reach a national audience, though you should always start locally. Your local media outlets should be interested in your book simply because of your geographic proximity. Every community loves local celebrities and now is your chance to become one where you live.

Assemble an Online Media List

To build your media contact list, visit the websites of all the local news stations, radio stations, newspapers, and magazines. You will want to contact editors and show producers who will be interested in your topic. If you have a business book, contact the business editor. If you have a cookbook, contact the features editor or lifestyles editor.

Use a spreadsheet or contact management system such as Microsoft Outlook to track your list of contacts. Make sure you include the following:

✓ Contact's name
✓ Title
✓ E-mail address
✓ Website address
✓ Phone number
✓ Special instructions for submitting news

In addition to the media outlets in your immediate area, spread out your list to those in large surrounding cities. If you come from a different area, locate the media outlets there too so you can tailor your pitch as a native of XYZ town. Certainly if your book is set in a particular city, you should make sure to contact every single media source in and around that city.

Create a separate list for national media contacts. Consider all of the major media outlets where you think your book would be of interest. Visit each website to gather the same information as you did for your local list.

Don't forget the nontraditional forms of media such as bloggers, podcasters, and Internet radio broadcasters.

Online Media Resources

✓ Radio Locator allows you to search for radio stations by location: radio-locator.com
✓ Radio Tower allows you to search for radio stations by format: radiotower.com
✓ WS Radio offers a host of online talk radio programs with a variety of topics: wsradio.com
✓ Blog Critics performs reviews of books and other media: blogcritics.org
✓ Women's Radio offers online talk radio programs for women with a variety of topics: womensradio.com
✓ All Talk Radio provides talk radio shows on a variety of subjects: alltalkradio.net/main
✓ The Midwest Book Review is a generous review service that favors self-published authors: midwestbookreview.com
✓ Online Newspapers provides a directory of newspapers by country and by state: onlinenewspapers.com

✓ Newspapers.com provides a directory of newspapers by country and state: newspapers.com

Leverage Press Releases

Once your media list is assembled, you should begin making contact. The most traditional way to do this is with a press release. These can be submitted directly to editors, reporters and producers. You can also search the websites for your targeted media outlets to find out if they have a general e-mail box or fax number where you can submit your release.

Reasons for Sending a Press Release

The mere fact that your book exists is usually not a good enough reason to send a press release. Remember, the media is there to share news with the public, not just to make you famous. Your release should never sound like a sales brochure for your book. If you want to receive media coverage, you have to create a newsworthy story or tie-in to current news or events.

Here are ten ways to make your press release newsworthy:

1. Relate your book to an upcoming holiday or anniversary.
2. Describe how your book solves a consumer problem.
3. Reveal results of a survey you have taken.
4. Announce a contest or winners of a contest.
5. Announce awards or recognition you have received.
6. Announce charitable or fund-raising activities.
7. Announce events you are hosting.
8. Take a controversial position on a hot topic related to your book.
9. Share details of a strategic partnership or alliance you have formed.
10. Offer something for free: product, service, demonstration, event, etc.

Bonus Benefit: Web Traffic

Press release distribution services, such as PRWeb.com, can push releases out to various Internet news services that get indexed by the search engines. Simply publishing a release with this service can boost Web traffic due to the number of links that point back to your site.

For maximum exposure, search engine optimization expert Jim Tendick advises that you can leverage PRWeb's SEO optimized distribution option (for a fee of $249). This service allows you to include anchored links (see Chapter 3 for an explanation) and can boost Web traffic temporarily. "It only works for about a month, but often a site can make it into the top ten [on the search engines]." This might be a viable option if you have a new book release or other timely reason that warrants a quick boost in Web traffic.

Writing Your Press Release

Follow these rules to write a press release that gets the attention you want:

✓ Read sample press releases before writing yours so you understand the proper format. Some good sources for locating professional releases are BusinessWire.com and PRNewswire.com.
✓ Start with a proper heading that includes your contact information. When listing phone numbers, indicate a day and evening number (reporters may call at odd hours) or simply list your cell phone number.
✓ Give the release an enticing title that captures the reader's interest and print it in bold type.
✓ Double space the body of your release for easy reading.
✓ The first paragraph should summarize the content by including the basics of who, what, where, when and why. You want to lay the foundation and include your hook immediately. Remember that you want to write engaging copy that prompts a response from the media.

✓ As awkward as it may be, it may be appropriate to quote yourself and write the release as if someone else has written it for you.

✓ Do not allow grammar or spelling mistakes to sneak into a press release. Make sure you edit your writing thoroughly and have a friend—or, better yet, two friends—review it for errors and content.

There are numerous services that you can pay to distribute your release to hundreds or thousands of markets. One of the most popular services is PRWeb (PRWeb.com). Whether or not you decide to pay for press release distribution, it's also a good idea to send the release out directly to appropriate media outlets from your media list.

Before you send your release, be sure you are prepared to answer interview questions. You may receive calls from reporters within a few hours of sending your release and will want to have thoughtful responses ready. Consider writing a list of points you want to make and keep it handy. I once sent out a press release and then headed to the mall. I ended up taking a twenty-minute interview with a reporter from the dressing room at Macy's.

Most people find that a press release can be worth its weight in gold since a news story usually generates more book sales than any form of paid advertising. Don't be discouraged if your first attempt doesn't receive the attention you want; simply try again until you find the formula and pitch that works.

Press Release Outline

For Immediate Release

Business Name
Address
Contact Person (You)
Day Phone
Evening Phone
E-mail

Catchy Headline Indicated In Bold Uppercase and Lowercase Letters

Date—City, State

Lead paragraph including summary of who, what, where, why and when.

Body of press release should include three to six paragraphs.

Include quotes from yourself or others (make sure to get their permission).

Paragraph Two

Paragraph Three

Paragraph Four

Paragraph Five

Write the content as if it were an article you were reading in a magazine. Don't forget to double space the text.

Develop a Media Pitch

I have personally sent out hundreds of press releases over the years. Though they can pay off and hit the media lottery, I've also had just as much success, possibly more, by contacting editors and reporters directly.

Media people are incredibly accessible because they rely on the public to locate stories. The contact information for reporters can often be found at the end of an article or on a publication's website. Editors are also listed on media websites.

You can write an e-mail to a reporter or editor anytime. One strategy you can use is to compliment a reporter on a story he wrote or tie a story in with your book. For example, Joe Reporter publishes an article in *Newsweek* about the dangers of day care centers. If you're the author of a book about child safety, you can write to Joe and let him know that you have ten great tips for keeping kids safe or that you are available as an expert source if he decides to write a follow-up article.

When I opened my bookstore in Sacramento, I wrote to the reporter for the *Sacramento Bee* who I noticed wrote several features on area businesses. I introduced myself, told the story of how

I left corporate America to open the bookstore, and offered to discuss my story with her if she was interested. Before I knew it, I received front section coverage, including several photos and an article so flattering that I couldn't have written it better myself.

Another strategy is to simply introduce yourself as a source. For example, if you are an expert in relationships, you can contact editors and reporters who cover this topic and let them know that you are available if they need a source for a future story. Be friendly, brief, and include a link to your press kit.

Recently, I came across a business columnist I hadn't seen before and quickly looked up her contact information. I sent a brief introduction along with a short blurb about my book. I let her know that I was available if she needed a quote from a small business expert. She sent me a quick "thanks" and said she was adding me to her database.

About four months later the reporter contacted me out of the blue. She interviewed me for not one, but two major articles in the same week—one in *Business Week* and another in the *Los Angeles Times*. Not bad for the five minutes it took me to send the message.

Though it can be time consuming to seek out reporters or editors one at a time, the results can make it worth your while. You never know when your timing might be perfect because the reporter was thinking about writing a story about your industry. And even if he doesn't want to write a story about you now, you could hear from him in three, six, or even twelve months after you make contact. Each message you send is like planting a seed. Some will grow, some won't. But you'll never know unless you try. Be sure to add each contact to your own media database so you can access the information when you need it again.

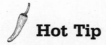 **Hot Tip**

Most major newspapers and magazines have daily or weekly e-mail newsletters. Consider subscribing to publications that cover your topic or area of interest. It only takes a minute to scan the newsletter for relevant topic ideas and you are quite likely to find inspiration and opportunity in doing so.

Book Reviews

Book reviews are always beneficial. Traditional book reviewers may not cover nonfiction, though you can certainly target journalists and media professionals who cover your area of interest.

For example, if you have a book about home decorating, you can target the editor of the lifestyle section of the newspaper, home improvement trade magazines, and websites and blogs that cover home improvement. In lieu of a review, you may spark interest in a feature story about you and your book or a journalist may want to quote you as an expert source for a future story.

If you want to avoid mailing out dozens of copies of your book, you can create a flyer that outlines the details of your book and estimated publication date. You can either include a tear-off coupon at the bottom of the flyer or insert a postage-paid postcard that the letter recipient can send back to request a complimentary review copy of your book.

Even easier, you can use e-mail to send out similar queries. All the recipient has to do is reply if he wants a copy. I have used both e-mail and direct mail with equally effective results—about 15 percent to 20 percent of recipients requested copies. Sending these inquiries led to a variety of opportunities including interviews for articles, book reviews, and offers to write articles for several publications.

Send your letter, via e-mail or direct mail, to the following sources (when relevant for your subject matter):

- ✓ Local bookstore owners or buyers
- ✓ Trade associations
- ✓ Specialty stores and gift shops
- ✓ Catalog companies (if your book would be a good fit for their readers)
- ✓ Media: newspaper editors or columnists, TV show producers, radio show producers
- ✓ Industry publications
- ✓ Website owners with a target audience that matches yours
- ✓ Bloggers

Send Galleys for Book Reviews

Some influential publications will only write book reviews from galley copies. A galley is an early edition of a book, often printed without complete editing and with a cover that simply has text with the title, author, publisher details, and estimated release date.

Many print shops can publish galley copies for you if your publisher can't. They will be more costly than your regular book since you only need a dozen or so copies, but they can be worth it if you can garner even one review from a major publication.

Galleys should be sent out four to six months prior to publication. Some of the large newspapers will also accept galleys for review. Check the website of each publication for submission guidelines. In most cases, you should include a press release or a data sheet about the book.

The following are influential industry magazines that accept galley copies:

✓ *Publishers Weekly*: publishersweekly.com
✓ *Library Journal*: libraryjournal.com
✓ *Kirkus Reviews*: kirkusreviews.com
✓ *ForeWord Magazine*: forewordmagazine.com

See "Resources" at the end of this book for additional book review outlets.

 **Hot Tip**

To locate reviewers of books in your genre, sign up for Google's Alert service (google.com). You can indicate keywords and Google will send you an e-mail when those keywords show up in the news or across the Internet. This is a great way to stay on top of your industry. I keep an alert for "business book review" so I can monitor book reviews and compile an ongoing list of reviewers and publications that review business books. I also set up an alert for my book title so I am notified when it is mentioned in the news, on blogs, and on other websites. Give it a try—it's free.

Contact Bloggers

Blogs are spreading like wildfire across the Internet and many bloggers have loyal and dedicated audiences for their daily messages. Contact bloggers who discuss topics related to your book and ask if they would be interested in receiving a review copy. A blogger with a big audience could bring you even more book sales than a standard book review. Many bloggers are signed up with Amazon.com's affiliate program and will happily promote your book along with a link so they can get a small piece of the pie.

To locate blogs and blog services, check out these sites:

✓ globeofblogs.com
✓ blogger.com
✓ blogsforsmallbusiness.com
✓ typepad.com
✓ blogcritics.com
✓ technorati.com/blogs

Radio Promotion

Promoting your book on the radio is one of the best ways to reach a broad audience. The biggest advantage? You never have to leave your home. Most radio shows will gladly host guests over the telephone. Program producers are also on the lookout for guests with interesting topics.

When you schedule an engagement, offer to provide the show with a list of sample interview questions that you are prepared to answer. Creating this list is an excellent way to prepare your answers ahead of time and reduce your nerves. Most radio producers and hosts will gladly accept your prepared questions. You can also offer several copies of your books as giveaways. Make it fun. Come up with a contest or quiz and give your books to people who call in with the right answer.

There are a number of ways to pitch your story to radio stations. You can send press releases or contact show producers individually. Show contact information and story submission procedures are listed on the websites of the biggest shows.

To get the most bang for your buck, target shows that are syndicated—meaning they are broadcast to multiple markets. But even a small radio show with a niche following can generate substantial book sales.

Make sure you are familiar with the show's format before wasting time on a pitch. A morning show program with two obnoxious disk jockeys is probably not likely to be interested in a political book unless you can find some funny or amusing way to tie it in with the format. Talk radio is the best format for most authors provided you can find a newsworthy angle or can show that there is a great interest in your topic for the general public or their specific audience demographic.

Here are some other methods for getting on the air:

> The *Radio-Television Interview Report* is a magazine used by show producers to book guests. You can advertise in this magazine for a fee if your budget allows. Visit rtir.com for details.
>
> Another fee-based service is radiotour.com. You can be listed in their online directory, have your press release distributed to over 1,000 shows and an e-mail sent to thousands of producers.
>
> Use the free directory on Gebbie Press (gebbieinc.com/radintro.htm) to locate radio stations all over the U.S.

Internet Radio

In addition to traditional radio, the Internet is exploding with online radio shows and podcasts. These interviews are conducted just like traditional radio shows, though often the host is also the producer.

One great advantage of Internet radio programs is that they are usually archived online so that you can continue to get exposure from listeners for a long, long time. Because of the diversity of the Internet, there are radio shows for virtually every topic you can imagine. From working moms and psychic healing to marketing and selling on eBay, there are shows available that should meet the needs of every author.

To locate Internet radio shows on your subject, start with a Google search on your primary keywords plus "radio show" or "radio." You might be surprised by the results you find. Here are some additional resources that host shows ranging from business and health to family matters and religion:

- ✓ wsradio.com
- ✓ contacttalkradio.com
- ✓ alltalkradio.net
- ✓ globaltalkradio.com
- ✓ webtalkradio.com
- ✓ blogtalkradio.com

Book Clubs

Word of mouth is some of the best kind of advertising that money can't buy. Many authors have found visiting book club meetings—where a number of people all read the same book and meet to discuss it—to be a worthwhile experience. Not only does it give you a chance to connect with readers, but you get to hear valuable feedback about your book.

Though many book clubs boast a small membership, sometimes just a dozen people or less, when you make an appearance those members are bound to talk about it with their friends and family. Plus, many book clubs advertise their book selections and events in a variety of venues.

Harper Collins Publishing believes in the value of visiting these meetings so much that the publisher has instituted a formal program where readers can request its authors call-in or visit their book club meetings.

To set this up yourself, you need to first locate book club groups and convince them to read your book. You might even offer one or more complimentary copies of your book as incentive. To locate clubs in your area, inquire at local bookstores or check the "Groups" section of craigslist.org or meetup.com. You can also indicate on your website that you are available to speak with book club groups.

Don't rule out book clubs outside of your area. You can visit them via conference call which can be almost as rewarding and certainly allows you to extend your reach.

Bulk Sales

Many authors get caught up in the whirlwind of book sales and promotion and focus on selling one copy at a time. If you want your book sales to soar, bulk sales can be a lucrative solution.

Your best bet is to focus on non-bookstore markets. Consider what kind of businesses your book might appeal to and then call, write, or show up and make your pitch. For example, if you have a book about aquariums, you could sell it to pet stores. If your book is about an historical event, you could offer it to museums, gift shops in the area featured in the book and historical societies.

Even if your target store doesn't typically offer books for sale, don't be afraid to approach them. Offer reasonable quantity discounts and if that doesn't work, you can consider offering a consignment agreement to test out the sales potential.

Here are some non-bookstore opportunities to consider:

Corporations: Many bulk sales deals have been struck at corporations. For example, *Who Moved My Cheese?* continues to be popular with the corporate market many years after it was on the best seller list. Corporations buy books to educate employees, as client giveaway items at conferences, for training purposes, etc.

Trade associations and chambers of commerce: Large organizations have been known to give away books as a benefit of membership or to offer them for sale to members.

Colleges: Your book doesn't have to be an official text book to be used by instructors or professors. If you can dazzle an instructor who has authority to select books, you can uncover a whole new market.

Catalogs: Thousands of mail order catalogs are distributed each year. Contact buyers for catalogs where you think your book would be a good fit.

Home shopping channels: Books periodically make it to home shopping channels. Check out QVC's submission process at www.qvcproductsearch.com.

eBay: This can be a surprisingly useful venue for selling off damaged copies of books, bulk quantities, or individual books. The added exposure can also be of value since you have the opportunity to reach a whole new audience.

Local businesses: In your local community, as an author you are often considered a local celebrity. Consider visiting gift shops, restaurants, independently-owned stores and any place that might be a good fit for your book.

Make sure you have in place a pricing schedule and a delivery method. If you don't self-publish, check to see if your publisher can drop-ship orders directly to buyers with the appropriate discount. If not, you need to make sure you have sufficient storage space and the ability to ship orders as needed.

Set up a quantity price break schedule. Here is copy that I have listed on the sales page for my business start-up book:

Quantity Discounts Available

Books are available for purchase by trade associations, businesses, retailers, schools, nonprofits and other organizations. Quantity price does not include shipping. Please contact us for a quote with shipping and include your address. Payment can be made with Paypal, check, money order, Visa or Mastercard.

Quantity	Discount	Cost Ea.
10-29	35%	$10.37
30-69	40%	$9.57
70-99	43%	$9.09
100-199	46%	$8.61
200+	50%	$7.98

Make More Money with Information Products

Once you build an audience for your book(s), you have an opportunity to make even more money. Your fans will be eager to purchase your future books, and will also be interested in other types of products.

Information products such as e-books, special reports, and teleseminars can be a fantastic source of revenue for authors. These products are most successful when they teach the buyer how to do something.

Following are some examples.

The author of a guide to fishing could also sell:

✓ A special report on the best fishing destinations in a specific state.
✓ A booklet about how to tie flies.
✓ An e-book with recipes for cooking fish.

The author of a children's book could also sell:

✓ An audio book version of the book.
✓ A companion workbook with fun activities for kids.
✓ An instructional report on how to help kids enjoy reading.

The author of a detective novel could also sell:

✓ A special report with alternate endings to the book.
✓ An e-book with short true crime stories.
✓ An instructional guide on how to write a detective novel.

The author of a business marketing book could also sell:

✓ An e-book with real-world marketing case studies.
✓ A workbook that helps readers develop a marketing plan.
✓ An instructional teleseminar that teaches listeners new marketing strategies.

Can you see how this strategy can help you generate extra income? I personally sell a variety of information products (this book was originally one of them.) For my business start-up book, I created a companion workbook. Since I used to own a bookstore, I wrote a workbook on how to start and run a used bookstore (incidentally this is one of my best-selling products primarily because it's a niche topic that few others have covered). I sell recordings to teleseminars that I've hosted and I also sell e-book versions of my books and special reports such as "100 Strategies for Business Networking and Strategic Alliances."

Not only can these products earn additional revenue, but they can attract new readers for your books. With every product you create, you also have a new marketing tool and reason to reach a new audience. You can use your website and electronic newsletter to market your products.

I also wrote an entire book on the subject: *From Entrepreneur to Infopreneur: Make Money with Books, E-books and Information Products*. If you would like to learn more, you can get details from my website at businessinfoguide.com/infopreneur.htm.

Book Events

The reality is that the average author sells six to eight books at a book signing event. Instead of holding a boring book signing where you sit at a table at the back of a bookstore and hope someone wanders over; consider turning your appearance into an event.

Here are some ideas:

✓ Host a reading (for fiction or children's authors).
✓ Give an informational talk.
✓ Have a theme, such as a luau or costume party, and make it fun for everyone.
✓ Team up with other authors to host a "local authors event."
✓ Give a demonstration related to the book.
✓ Give away prizes (these attract people).
✓ Provide fun activities and games for kids (parents love this).

✓ Team up to support a local charity and tie it in to your event.
✓ Offer food and beverages.
✓ Enlist your friends and colleagues to help.
✓ Leverage a gimmick or prop like a live petting zoo or a series of costume changes.

Francine Silverman is an author and the founder of BookPromotionNewsletter.com, a resource for learning about book promotion. "The most books I ever sold happened during my book launch party for my book, *Talk Radio for Authors*, at a radio studio in Manhattan," says Silverman. "The host interviewed the guests for his Internet TV show, which everyone enjoyed. Even though the event cost me money for the food and wine, it was the best promotional idea I've ever had."

The point is that book signings don't draw a crowd unless you are famous, so if you can find new and innovative ways to get people to take the time to show up, not only will you sell more books, but you'll also have a good time.

Author Interview

Author: Jill Lublin

Books: *Guerrilla Publicity* and *Networking Magic*

Website: jilllublin.com

What is your book about?

Guerrilla Publicity is about how to get more visibility and credibility without spending a fortune. *Networking Magic* is about how to connect effectively and create positive results in your relationships.

What led you to publish the book?

I wanted to put my expertise into an avenue that would reach more people.

How has being an author changed or improved your life personally or professionally?

It has expanded every area of my life. It put me more in the public eye. I am more able to live my purpose every day and help people get their message out.

What online marketing methods have worked best for you?

Affiliate marketing [Having other people sell your books and earn commission].

Do you have a favorite off-line book marketing strategy?

Ongoing publicity.

Do you own a business?

Yes. Promising Promotion is a strategic consulting firm that helps business owners, consultants, speaker, and authors to get their word out and increase visibility in the marketplace.

Has being an author helped your business in any way?

It increased my credibility. It also allowed me to increase my fees by leveraging my expertise.

If you were just getting started in publishing today, is there anything that you would do differently?

I would have done it sooner.

How do you view the advantages or disadvantages of self publishing vs. traditional publishing?

Self publishing is a rougher road. Aside from a time stand-point of having to do everything yourself, it is very expensive. With traditional publishing, you still have a lot of work to do and will have costs, but it is far less. An important thing to remember with traditional publishing is—just because you have a publisher, don't expect to be in every bookstore—you still have your own leg work to do to get the word out right along with them.

What advice do you have for other authors?

Start your publicity campaign a year before the book is published. Be willing to be bold about getting your message out. Don't make your message all about your book—be newsworthy. Offer the public solutions by finding real new angles.

CHAPTER 8

Amazon.com Success Strategies

As a former owner of an independent bookstore, I do my best to support small stores. But I will admit that even when I owned a store and had access to my choice of over 30,000 books, I still found myself drawn to—and placing frequent orders with—Amazon.com.

Amazon is a true reader's paradise and so far nobody is doing a better job of selling books online. I personally love the reader recommendations, the links to related books, the ability to perform keyword searches, and the fact that I can post and read reviews. I can get lost on Amazon for hours.

As an author, there are many ways to ratchet up your Amazon.com sales. The company continues to release innovative tools for site users and authors to promote books. It's getting hard to keep up with all of the bells and whistles available on Amazon, but there are some key strategies that authors can use to leverage this online superstore and boost book sales. This chapter covers the most commonly used methods.

Your Amazon Profile

If you have an account with Amazon.com, you have the ability to set up a public profile. These profiles can be quite useful for authors since it's another way to communicate with the reading public. I have personally received e-mails from readers as a result of having my profile available.

To access your profile, you can click on the link in the upper right on the Amazon screen, or use this one: amazon.com/gp/pdp/profile/.

You can edit your profile to include as much or as little information as you want to share with the public. The "About Me" section down on the left allows you to post the following information:

✓ **Your Name**.

✓ **Your Website Address**—List your link. This is a great advantage.

✓ **Your E-mail Address**—You can decide whether or not you want this to be publicly viewable. I choose to hide mine in an effort to minimize spam messages.

✓ **Your Amazon Signature**—This is displayed with your name anytime you post a book review or create a recommended reading list. Your signature can include details about you and your book. For example, my signature is: *Small Business Expert, Author of 'The Business Startup Checklist' & 'From Entrepreneur to Infopreneur,' Founder of BusinessInfoGuide.com.*

✓ **Your Birthday**—You're not required to list a year, nor are you required to make this public at all. I figured it wouldn't hurt anything to display mine and got a great laugh when one of my readers sent me a birthday greeting and I had to ask how she knew.

✓ **Your Interests**—Amazon will allow you to enter up to 4,000 characters of text describing your interests. This is a great opportunity to inject some personality into your profile and talk about subjects related to your book(s).

✓ **Your Biography**—Opportunity knocks since you can share anything you want your readers to know about you. Don't forget to include another link to your website—it can't hurt.

Your profile page also serves as a dashboard where you can view, create, and change your Amazon Blog/Plog entries, Listmania lists, So You'd Like To guides, and more.

Listmania Lists

Listmania lists are displayed throughout Amazon.com alongside book search results and at the bottom of the page when displaying a book. These lists are compiled by Amazon users as a way to share their favorite titles.

As an author, you can create lists and even include your own book title. The advantage is that your list will appear alongside the other books you include in the list, and Amazon surfers can be introduced to your title as a result.

For example, if you have a book about how to sell on eBay, you can compile a Listmania list of up to forty books that are also related to selling on eBay. The goal is to give your book more exposure with Amazon customers who are looking for books on the same subject.

To create a list, you can start from your profile page on Amazon or from any page displaying a book—click on the "Create a Listmania List" link. You give your list a title and fill in the box for your qualifications such as "Author of XYZ book."

You are allowed to write an introduction for your list, and this is a fantastic opportunity to write a quick paragraph about who you are and what you do. Then you list the ISBN numbers for each book. You can include a comment about each book if you like, but this is not mandatory.

Once approved, your list will appear across Amazon when books from your list are displayed. You never know when your book might catch the interest of someone browsing your list.

So You'd Like To Guides

Similar to Listmania Lists, So You'd Like To guides provide a method for recommending books. The difference is that these guides are more text-intensive so when you create a guide, you are expected to include plenty of commentary or instruction.

For example, if you are the author of a cookbook, you could create a guide called, "So You'd Like to Learn How to Cook Like a Pro." In it you could describe different cooking methods along with your book and other books that you want to feature.

I like to use reprints of my how-to articles to write these guides. I created a guide called, "So You'd Like to Become a Mompreneur" which includes an article I wrote that outlines some business options for moms, and at the bottom is a list of related books. You can see it for yourself here: amazon.com/gp/richpub/syltguides/ fullview/R3GHTQWA65BLC7/ref=cm_sylt_pdp_title_full_1.

To create a guide, you can start from your profile page on Amazon or from any page displaying a book—click on the "Create a So You'd Like To Guide."

Amazon Connect

This unique program allows authors to post brief messages to readers. Amazon Connect messages will appear:

✓ On the Amazon home page of everyone who has ever bought your book
✓ On your book's detail page
✓ On your author profile page

The purpose of this program is to allow authors to communicate with readers and develop their fan base. You can update readers with news about what you're up to, new projects you are working on, scheduled public appearances, awards or recognition you've received, and anything else you feel like sharing.

There is no cost to join this program and requires a simple registration and approval process. You can sign up by visiting: amazon.com/connect.

You can also choose to simply post messages to your Amazon Blog. Visit your profile page to add new entries.

If you would like to see an example, you can view my Amazon Connect messages for my book *The Business Startup Checklist and Planning Guide* by searching Amazon for the book title. If you're already on Amazon.com shopping, you have probably noticed many authors taking advantage of this great feature.

Search Inside the Book

Amazon's Search Inside this Book program allows shoppers to view content within your book including the table of contents and the majority of the text in your book. Some authors worry that they will be giving away their books by participating in this program. I disagree. This is an excellent way to assist potential buyers in making the decision to purchase your book. This program allows potential buyers to get a better idea of the content in your book and can ultimately lead to a sale. The program is also safe—shoppers cannot copy your text or print the pages.

Your publisher will likely submit your book for this program for you. If you are self-published, go to your book's page on Amazon and locate the link below the book image that says "Publisher: Learn how customers can search inside this book." This will walk you through the process of submitting your request to Amazon. Once approved, you will be asked to mail in a copy of your book so it can be scanned into the system.

Amazon Associates

The Associates program is Amazon's affiliate system and it allows you to earn a commission when you recommend books to others for purchase. You can generate links, product ads, and other banner-type ads that you can insert onto pages in your website. When a user clicks through to Amazon and makes a purchase, you earn a percentage of the sale. Better yet, you earn a percentage of the buyer's entire transaction, not just for the book you recommended.

This can be a useful tool if you enjoy recommending books to others. For example, if you frequently recommend books in your electronic newsletter, you could embed the Amazon link so that you earn commission when your readers heed your advice and buy the book.

If you don't want to sell your own books directly, this program can give you a simple way to sell your books from your website by simply directing buyers to Amazon.

There is no cost to join, though you are required to fill out an application. Once approved, you will be able to login to your Associates account and generate links or review sales reports. Amazon pays commission on a monthly basis.

To sign up, visit: affiliate-program.amazon.com/gp/associates/join.

Amazon Advantage Program

This program is for independent publishers who want to list their titles directly on Amazon. It costs under $30 per year and you must agree to a 55 percent discount on your book(s)—this is the fee that Amazon keeps as its commission. Incidentally, this is a relatively standard discount that wholesalers to bookstores expect off the cover price of a book. This is why it is so important for self-published authors to price their books correctly and leave enough room to make a profit.

The biggest benefit is that Amazon will agree to stock your book and make it available to its massive customer base. However, don't expect to list your book with Amazon and watch sales soar. You still have plenty of marketing work to do in order to make your book stand out in a marketplace with millions of other books.

If you're interested in joining the Advantage program, visit: advantage.amazon.com/gp/vendor/public/join-advantage-books.

Search Suggestions

You have the power to suggest search terms to be associated with your book. Search terms are essentially the keywords that readers use to locate your book. Amazon automatically indexes the title of your book and some of the book description, but you can make sure that specific topics or themes from the book are also included when Amazon shoppers perform a book search.

For example, if you have a book about nutrition, you could add the following search terms:

- ✓ Trans-fats
- ✓ Cholesterol
- ✓ Vitamins
- ✓ Proper eating

✓ Weight management
✓ Weight loss
✓ Protein
✓ Carbohydrates

To submit search terms, simply go to your book's page on Amazon and scroll down to the heading "Help Others Find This Item," then click on "Make a Search Suggestion." You can enter one search term at a time and must also write a brief explanation about why this term is appropriate for the book.

Using the example above, if you want to submit "Trans-fats," your explanation might be, "There is an entire chapter in this book devoted to trans-fats."

Once your search suggestion is approved, Amazon will then include your book in search results when your search terms are used. This is a valuable opportunity to expand your book's reach so make sure you spend some time identifying appropriate search terms for your book.

Book Reviews

Amazon book reviews are a tool for readers to post feedback on titles. These reviews are rated on a starred system, from one to five stars, and include space to write a detailed written review.

Most authors believe that these reviews impact book sales. I know that I read them when making buying decisions. It is certainly worthwhile to solicit reviews for your book. You can start by asking everyone you know. Family, friends, colleagues, business partners and fellow trade association members can all log on to Amazon and help your position by posting favorable reviews. You likely will receive reviews from your reading audience too.

Dan Poynter, author of *The Self-Publishing Manual*, allows authors to post requests for Amazon reviews in his e-zine. You can sign up for his newsletter (which is also an excellent resource for authors and publishers) at parapublishing.com. You must agree to send free review copies to all who reply to your post.

Don't be afraid to ask for reviews. Most people are happy to write them. I know one author who set up an Internet terminal at his book launch party and encouraged attendees to log on to Amazon right there on the spot. Whenever I receive e-mail from readers who write to thank me or offer praise for one of my books, I send a gracious reply and request that the reader take a moment to post a similar comment on Amazon.

Reviewing Other People's Books

You can also post reviews for other people's books on Amazon. The benefit is that this is another way to get your name out in the reading community. Amazon reviews include the name of the reviewer, along with a link back to the reviewer's profile page. In addition to your name, the signature that you set up in your profile page is also included with your review.

When reviewing books, seek out titles that reach the same target audience as your book. Make sure you have actually read the book you are reviewing. I would also recommend that you do your best to post favorable reviews. Negative reviews can adversely affect book sales and that author may come back to find you and return the sentiment by posting a nasty review of your book.

You might also be surprised to receive a thanks-for-your-review message from the author of the book. I have been known to write these in response to good reviews when the writer's e-mail address is readily available. I have also received these types of thank you messages. As an avid reader, I find it easy to take a moment to post praise for a book I genuinely enjoyed. I also try to get the most out of everything I write, so my reviews also end up in my electronic newsletter and on my blog.

Get Your Book Reviewed by Amazon

Ask your publisher if they plan to submit your book to Amazon for review and if not, consider doing this yourself. Amazon.com employs category editors who may review your book which will assist with its promotion. They will not guarantee a review or even notify you of receipt of the book, but it's worth the price of postage to submit your book along with any promotional materials to:

Editorial Department
Category Editor (i.e. Travel Editor)
Amazon.com
705 5th Ave. South, 5th floor
Seattle, WA 98104

There is very little you can do to follow up with the Amazon editor other than wait and check your book's details page for updates.

Selling E-books on Amazon

If you don't own the e-book rights for your book, you can skip this section. Otherwise, e-book publishers should flag this page for reference.

Since Amazon.com acquired Mobipocket in April 2005, the online bookseller has made some dramatic changes to its e-book strategy. Publishers and authors used to be required to set up an account with Lightning Source to list e-books with Amazon, but now e-books are managed by Mobipocket.

To complicate matters further, the e-book version of a title is no longer listed with its print version. In fact, Amazon no longer indexes e-books on its site at all. When you browse Amazon's book categories and click on "e-books," you are directed to a link that takes you out of Amazon.com and onto Mobipocket.com. The reality is that e-books are no longer actually sold on Amazon.com at all, but directly through its subsidiary.

There is a debate brewing on blogs across cyberspace about this controversial strategy since many consumers prefer the old method of purchasing e-books directly from Amazon. But unless Amazon decides to change its strategy again, publishers and authors must follow the new policy to list their e-books for sale.

Amazon would like to manage the process of approving e-book publishers and asks publishers to send an e-mail to digitalrights@amazon.com with the following information:

> What publishing company do you represent? (If you are the author, please enter "author" and the name of the publishing company you work with)

Your contact information:

Name:

Professional title:

Business address:

E-mail address:

Phone number:

Please list the ISBNs of the books you are considering making available as e-books:

For these titles listed, do you own the digital rights (rights to sell books in a digital format)?

Several days after receipt of this information, Amazon will send you an e-mail with further instructions for registering a publisher account with Mobipocket. But you can jump ahead in the process by following these steps:

1. Register your publisher account: mobipocket.com/e-bookBase/en/Homepage/apply.asp?Type=Publisher.

2. Review and sign the publisher agreement: mobipocket.com/e-bookBase/en/Homepage/pub_agreement.asp.

3. Fax the agreement back to Mobipocket in France at 33 148 25 90 07. According to the digital rights staff at Amazon, this is the only method that is available for returning signed agreements (they won't accept agreements via e-mail). Following receipt of your signed agreement, Mobipocket will send you an e-mail with an account login and password.

4. While you wait for your login information, you can convert your e-books to Mobipocket format. Download the free conversion software at: mobipocket.com/en/DownloadSoft/ProductDetailsCreator.asp?edition=Publisher.

The program can convert MS Word, text, or PDF documents. Be sure to examine your newly created e-book with Mobipocket's preview tool since the formatting does not always convert correctly. You may need to make some adjustments to text spacing or font sizes.

5. As soon as you receive your login information for your publisher account, you can manage your publisher account at mobipocket.com/e-bookbase/en/homepage/Logon.asp.

This is where you will upload your e-book and set your desired retail price. Keep in mind that Mobipocket retains 50 percent of the retail price as their royalty payment. You will also give up another 10 percent of the price if you allow affiliate sales.

6. Once you have verified that the e-book looks good and your price is set, you must choose to activate the file. This process makes the e-book available to buyers at Mobipocket.com and through their network of partners. Conversely, if you want to remove your e-book from Mobipocket's catalog, you can deselect the "activate" option.

Though many of us would like the ability to submit e-books in PDF format, as well as see e-book titles listed with their print counterparts on Amazon, for now we can only hope that Amazon modifies its process in the near future. In the meantime, the Mobipocket publisher account costs nothing to implement and the listing process, though tedious, is relatively easy to complete. Perhaps with Mobipocket's network of partners, the extra effort will be worthwhile when it comes time to receive royalty payments for our e-book sales.

Amazon Kindle

As this book was going to press, the publishing world was buzzing about Amazon's latest offering. Kindle is a wireless, portable reading device that allows users to download books, blogs, magazines, and newsletters for reading on a digital screen.

Like all new technology (iPods, for example) the price for the Kindle device is currently on the high end (about $400), but that isn't deterring avid readers. One of the most attractive features is the instant gratification of purchasing a Kindle edition of a book from Amazon and then wirelessly downloading it in a matter of minutes.

Though it's a bit early to tell if Kindle has staying power, if the number of product reviews (in the thousands) is an indication, Kindle is likely to stick around.

The big publishing houses are making their books available to Kindle buyers. If you are a self-publisher, you can upload your book for free through Amazon's Digital Text Platform. Instructions are available at http://dtp.amazon.com.

E-mail Campaigns

One method for generating book sales is to implement an e-mail marketing campaign. Aside from your own mailing list, you should contact your peers and ask them to participate. Some authors have had tremendous success with these kinds of marketing efforts, so much so that they have seen their books skyrocket to the top of Amazon.com's best-sellers list.

Here are the steps to follow to make this strategy work for you:

✓ Make a list of the people you know and even those that you don't who have significant mailing list databases. Anyone who works in your general industry and reaches your target audience can participate in a campaign like this.

✓ Select a date for your campaign on or shortly after the official release of your book.

✓ Compile a list of bonus products you will give away to each person who purchases your book on the designated date. Bonus products can include electronic downloads, teleseminar admission, booklets, free consulting time, and any other kind of information product.

✓ Contact each person on your list and ask them to participate in your book launch campaign by agreeing to take two actions: Provide a product that you will give away as a bonus with purchase and agree to send an e-mail to their contact database on the date you've selected. Your peers should be interested in participating because this equates to free promotion for them too. If ten contacts send out e-mails to each of their databases, and those databases each have 10,000 subscribers, each participant has a chance to get their name in front of 100,000 people.

Here is a sample e-mail invitation:

Dear <colleague's name>,

You may have heard by now that I have a new book coming out in June called *From Entrepreneur to Infopreneur: Make Money with Books, E-books and Information Products*. I am excited about the release of this book and am writing to invite you to participate in a special e-mail launch campaign.

How it works:
Campaign Date: June 25

I am asking you and several other industry experts to each contribute a bonus product (such as an e-book or special report) that customers will receive as a reward for purchasing my book on the campaign date. Your product will be promoted along with your name and website link throughout the e-mail campaign, thus creating tremendous exposure for you.

As a campaign participant, you agree to send a special e-mail out to your mailing list on the morning of June 25 (or the evening of June 24) describing the special offer and inviting your subscribers to participate (I will send you a draft of the e-mail).

I will set up a special Web page that lists all of the bonus products, participants and their websites, and a complete description of the promotion. When a customer purchases my book from Amazon.com on June 25, he can then forward the receipt to me and I will send him the entire set of bonus products.

If you would like to contribute a product and participate in the e-mail campaign, please send me your bonus product in PDF or other format, along with a brief description of the product and its value, no later than May 30.

Please let me know if you have any questions. I appreciate your consideration and hope to hear from you soon.

Warm regards,
Stephanie Chandler

✓ Set up a page on your website with complete details about the special offer. Be sure to include links to websites for each participant who contributes a product for your campaign.

✓ Assemble the e-mail copy for your campaign team to use to send to their mailing list subscribers. The message should include details about the one-day only offer, a list of the bonus products readers will receive, a link to your website page that gives a complete overview of the offer, and instructions for redeeming the offer for bonus products.

Sample E-mail Copy:

Dear Friend,

I have a special offer for you that is valid for one day only. My colleague, Stephanie Chandler, is releasing her powerful new book, *From Entrepreneur to Infopreneur: Make Money with Books, E-books, and Information Products*. If you want to learn how to create information products and sell them for a profit, add revenue streams to your existing business, create products for back of the room sales, or launch a new business selling information, then this is the book for you.

The Offer:

If you purchase this book today, you will receive several hundred dollars worth of bonus products. Here's a list of what you will get:

✓ *Joe Author's 32-page e-book "Marketing Mania"—a $30 value! (link to Joe's website)*

✓ *Famous Fred's 15-page special report "Kick-Butt Sales Strategies"—a $15 value! (link to Fred's website)*

✓ *Admission to Susie Seller's teleseminar "How to Generate Online Promotions"—worth $29.95! (link to Susie's website)*

✓ *Annie Author's list of 500 media contacts—a $99 value! (Annie's website)*

✓ *Edna Entrepreneur's subscription newsletter for six months—worth $29! (Edna's website)*

✓ *Consulting time with Susie Speaker—30 minutes worth $75!*
  (Susie's website)
✓ *Etc...*

How It Works:

Place your order TODAY ONLY through Amazon.com (insert link to Amazon). Forward your purchase receipt to (your e-mail address) and Stephanie will send you all of these bonus products within twenty-four hours. It's that easy!

This is a great offer that you don't want to miss. Here is what some reviewers are saying about Stephanie's new book:

(insert endorsements)

This offer is valid for today only so don't wait! Order your copy now (you can thank me later!).
(insert Amazon link again).

Best regards,
Joe Participant

Don't forget to send a reminder to your campaign team on the morning that the campaign is scheduled to occur. Also, plan to spend the day at your computer watching your sales rank improve on Amazon and delivering e-mails with bonus products to everyone that purchases your book.

Author Interview

Author: Barbara Winter

Most recent book: *Making a Living Without a Job*

Total # of books published: Two and a third coming out in late 2007 which is tentatively titled *Self-employment Rocks!*

Website: barbarawinter.com

What is your book about?

It's a handbook for creative self-employment that not only is about how to get started, but how to keep going.

What led you to publish the book?

I knew that I had an approach to self-employment that wasn't being written about, but the real impetus was the popularity of my seminars on the same subject. I am especially interested in the role of inspiration in creating a successful small business and wasn't seeing that addressed by other startup manuals.

How has being an author changed or improved your life personally or professionally?

I think anytime we take on a new project and it succeeds it adds to our self-confidence. It also has opened doors to other invitations and opportunities.

What online marketing methods have worked best for you?

It always is terrific when someone else recommends my books, but having a website with informational and inspirational articles also, I suspect, gives people a glimpse of what they might expect from a book I've written.

Do you have a favorite off-line book marketing strategy?

I really enjoy doing radio interviews and that often has a nice impact on sales. Lately, I've been doing quite a few interviews that are being used on podcasts.

And I hand-sell an enormous number of books through my seminars.

Do you own a business?

My business, Winning Ways, is a collection of products and events all designed to help people become inspired entrepreneurs. In fact, spreading entrepreneurial spirit in any possible way I can is my major passion. I see business as a creative experience and so my mission is to help entrepreneurs be more artistic and help artists be more entrepreneurial.

Has being an author helped your business in any way?

It all flows together.

If you were just getting started in publishing today, is there anything that you would do differently?

I got into publishing through the back door and because I had created a bit of visibility through my seminars and some interviews that went out on the wire services, I had three publishers that solicited me. Fortunately, I was ready and had a book proposal written.

I got published without benefit of an agent and if I were to do a book that would be published by a conventional publisher, I think I'd want to work with an agent for that.

Do you have any favorite online resources or websites that you would like to recommend?

I'm a huge fan of John Kremer's book marketing advice. He has several websites including bookmarket.com. His weekly mailings of book marketing tips are terrific.

What advice do you have for other authors?

Be willing to be an active participant in marketing your books. I think I had the naive notion that if a big publisher was doing my books, they'd really promote them. Not really. In fact, one of the editors who offered me a contract did so after attending a seminar and watching me speak. So publishers assume that authors will be involved, but authors don't always know that.

Most of all, have fun with your life as an author and try lots of different things. You never know where your next reader may be coming from.

Final Thoughts

I hope that you found many ideas in this book to improve your position as an author and to increase your overall success. I enjoyed interviewing the authors who are profiled here as I love to learn from the real-world success of others. I will continue this quest and will share the details in my future books (new book ideas are brewing every day).

As mentioned earlier, the Internet is continuing to evolve. More and more opportunities are being introduced that authors can leverage to build a platform and sell more books. I will continue researching these opportunities and will make articles and updates available through my website, newsletter and blog. Please be sure to stop by and visit.

I also welcome your feedback and new ideas. Please send me your thoughts anytime to BookUpdate@BusinessInfoGuide.com.

I am reminded daily that I am fortunate to be an author and to have a platform to share what I am learning along the way. Not everyone can accomplish what we have as authors—it is no easy task to write a complete book and then find a home for it. So whether you are working on your first book or your twentieth, I encourage you to *persevere*—and don't forget to have some fun along the way.

Thank you for your time and support. I wish you wild success in all of your publishing endeavors!

Directory of Resources

Printed Bookmarks, Postcards, Business Cards, and Brochures

Your printed materials can be invaluable promotional tools. Make sure you have a quality image of your book cover and use it on all of your correspondence. Bookmarks can be handed out at every event and left in bookstores. Postcards and brochures can be mailed out to customers, media, bookstores, businesses, and everyone you can think of. Business cards should be given to everyone you encounter. You can even stuff any of these items into remittance envelopes when you pay your bills.

Microsoft Publisher is an excellent tool for designing these yourself, but you can also elect to hire a graphic designer if your budget allows. Send a request for quote (RFQ) to all local print shops to compare pricing. Printing locally will save you on shipping, though you may also want to check the prices of some of the online companies:

- ✓ VistaPrint.com
- ✓ iPrint.com
- ✓ GotPrint.com
- ✓ Tu-Vets.com
- ✓ Separacolor.com

Trade Shows & Conferences

The industry's largest publishing tradeshow is Book Expo America: bookexpoamerica.com. All kinds of publishing industry professionals turn out for this multi-day event including publishers, agents, authors, booksellers, retailers, librarians, and others. BEA provides excellent opportunities for learning and networking.

Shaw Guides offers a comprehensive list of writer's conferences around the world: writing.shawguides.com.

WC&C provides another good list of writer's conferences: writersconf.org.

Book Marketing Resources

John Kremer hosts one of the most comprehensive websites available for book marketing tips and resources: bookmarket.com.

Dan Poynter hosts one of the best newsletters for authors, both self-published and traditionally published: parapublishing.com.

Francine Silverman publishes *The Book Promotion Newsletter* which is loaded with reader tips and experiences: book—promotionnewsletter.com.

Book Review Sources

The following are some other sources to send your book for review:

Book Links (American Library Association magazine): ala.org/ala/productsandpublications/periodicals/booklinks/booklinks.htm

Booklist (American Library Association magazine): ala.org/ala/booklist/booklist.htm

BookPage: bookpage.com

Children's Bookwatch (Midwest Book Review): midwestbookreview.com/cbw

ForeWord Magazine: forewordmagazine.com

Heartland Reviews: heartlandreviews.com

Horn Book Magazine (children's book reviews): hbook.com

Independent Publisher Magazine: independentpublisher.com

Internet Bookwatch (*Midwest Book Review*): midwestbookreview.com/ibw

Kirkus Reviews: kirkusreviews.com/kirkusreviews/index.jsp

Library Journal: libraryjournal.com

Library Media Connection: linworth.com/lmc.html

Los Angeles Times Magazine: latimes.com/features/printedition/magazine

Midwest Book Review: midwestbookreview.com (They are especially considerate of independent publishers.)

New York Times Book Review: nytimes.com/pages/books

Publishers Weekly: publishersweekly.com

School Library Journal: schoollibraryjournal.com

Small Press Bookwatch (Midwest Book Review): midwestbookreview.com/sbw

Small Press Review: dustbooks.com/sprinfo.htm

The Boston Book Review: bookwire.com/bookwire/bbr/bbr-home.html

Washington Post Book World: washingtonpost.com/wp-dyn/content/print/bookworld/index.html

Online Newsletters and Resources for Writers

Writers Weekly offers resources for magazine markets and self-published books: writersweekly.com.

Writers Net is for writers, editors, agents, and publishers and includes discussion forums: writers.net.

Media Bistro targets anyone who deals with content: writers, publishers, editors, etc. and offers forums, media events, and other writing-related resources: mediabistro.com.

Absolute Write offers freelance markets and information for authors: absolutewrite.com.

Publisher's Marketplace provides publishing industry news and resources for publishers, editors, and agents: publishersmarketplace.com.

Para Publishing is Dan Poynter's site for self-publishers. His weekly newsletter is loaded with tips and information: parapublishing.com.

For Freelancers

If you are interested in freelance writing (getting paid to write for magazines), the following are resources for you:

Writer's Market is a subscription-based service from the folks at Writer's Digest that allows you to search for market information for consumer and trade magazines, newspapers, and literary agents: writersmarket.com.

Funds for Writers details paying freelance writing markets and weekly newsletter: fundsforwriters.com.

Freelance Success is a subscription-based service with online forums for sharing market info and advice. Writers on this forum command $1+ per word and write for the big national publications: freelancesuccess.com.

Writer's Magazines

The following are the most popular print magazines available:

Writer's Digest: writersdigest.com
The Writer: writermag.com
Poets & Writers Magazine: pw.org
ByLine Magazine: bylinemag.com

Publisher's Weekly is a publishing industry standard for learning about trends in the marketplace: publishersweekly.com. Because the subscription price is hefty, you may want to read this one at your local library. There is no charge to subscribe to their e-zine.

Writer's Associations

Associations for writers provide a wonderful way to network with other writers and access resources. These associations are abundant and many have regional chapters. Most require membership dues ranging from $30 to $200. Evaluate several associations and then decide which ones fit your needs best. You may even want to join more than one.

The following are some associations to consider:

Small Publisher's Association of North America: spannet.org

PMA, The Independent Publisher's Association: PMA-online.org

Small Publishers, Artists, and Writers Network: spawn.org

American Society of Journalists and Authors: asja.org

Association of Authors and Publishers: authorsandpublishers.org

Directory and Database Publishers Forum & Network: dpfn.com

National Association of Women Writers: nationalwriters.com

National Writer's Association: nationalwriters.com

The following are associations with a regional focus:

Arizona Book Publishing Association: azbookpub.com

Bay Area Independent Publishers Association: baipa.org

Book Publishers Northwest: bpnw.org

Colorado Independent Publishers Association: cipa-books.com

Connecticut Authors and Publishers Association: aboutcapa.com

Florida Publishers Association: flbookpub.org

Illinois Women's Press Association: iwpa.org

Independent Writers of Southern California: iwosc.org

Minnesota Book Publishers Round Table: publishersroundtable.org

New Mexico Book Association: nmbook.org

Northern California Publishers & Authors: norcalpa.org

Publishers Association of the South: pubsouth.org

St. Louis Publishers Association: stlouispublishers.org

Wisconsin Regional Writers Association: wrwa.net
Writers League of Texas: writersleague.org

The above list is just a sampling of the regional writer's trade associations. Use the internet and a keyword search to local additional organizations in your area. More associations are also listed at businessinfoguide.com/publishing.htm.

Domain Registration and Hosting Services

Yahoo!: smallbusiness.yahoo.com
Go Daddy: godaddy.com
Network Solutions: networksolutions.com
Geocities: geocities.yahoo.com
Readyhosting.com

Other Website Service Providers

The Template Store: thetemplatestore.com—Provides pre-designed templates you can manage with Microsoft Frontpage or Dreamweaver.
Paymentech: paymentech.net— Merchant card processing service.
Paypal: paypal.com—Merchant card processing, payment collection, and Web site shopping cart solutions.
1Shopping Cart: 1shoppingcart.com—Merchant card processing, auto responders, and comprehensive shopping cart solutions.
Payloadz: payloadz.com—Shopping cart solution for selling and delivering electronic content such as e-books and special reports.
The Frontpage Resource site offers all kinds of tips, tutorials and tricks if you get stuck: accessfp.net.

E-book Publishing

Payloadz: payloadz.com
Microsoft Reader: microsoft.com/reader/developers/downloads/rmr.asp

Mobipocket Reader: mobipocket.com
Palm Reader: e-books.palm.com/product/detail/19286
Hie-book Reader: hie-book.com
Adobe Reader: adobe.com/products/acrobat/readstep2.html
Adobe Acrobat (PDF creator): adobe.com
E-book Edit Pro: e-bookedit.com
Desktop Author: desktopauthor.com
Activ E-book Compiler: e-bookcompiler.com
E-book Generator: e-bookgenerator.com
eCover Creator: logocreator.com
eCover Generator: ecovergenerator.com
Lightning Source (LSI): LightningSource.com
Yahoo Group for E-book Publishing: groups.yahoo.com/
    group/e-book-community
E-book Mall: e-bookmall-publishing.com
E-books 'N Bytes: e-booksnbytes.com

Shipping Service Providers

United States Post Office: usps.gov
United Parcel Service: ups.com
Federal Express: fedex.com
Uline (supplies): uline.com
Papermart (supplies): papermart.com
Small Business Warehousing (fulfillment service):
    sbwarehousing.com
Ship SMO (fulfillment service): shipsmo.com
Specialty Fulfillment Center (fulfillment service):
    pickandship.com

Resources for Professional Speaking

SpeakerNetNews: speakernetnews.com
Speaker Match: speakermatch.com
BusinessInfoGuide: businessinfoguide.com/speaking.htm
Learning Annex: learningannex.com
Toastmasters: toastmasters.com

National Speakers Association: nsaspeaker.org
Professional Speakers Association: professionalspeakers.org
The Jokes: the-jokes.com
Jokes: jokes.com
Quotations: quotationspage.com

Books

1001 Ways to Market Your Books for Authors and Publishers, John Kremer
The Complete Guide to Book Marketing, David Cole
Damn. Why Didn't I Write That? How Ordinary People Are Raking in $100,000.00...Or More Writing Nonfiction Books & How You Can Too, Marc McCutcheon
Dan Poynter's The Self Publishing Manual, Dan Poynter
The Fast Track Course on How to Write a Nonfiction Book Proposal, Stephen Blake Mettee
From Entrepreneur to Infopreneur: Make Money with Books, E-Books and Information Products, Stephanie Chandler
Guerrilla Marketing for Writers: 100 Weapons to Help You Sell Your Work, Jay Conrad Levinson, Rick Frishman, and Michael Larsen
The New Influencers: A Marketer's Guide to the New Social Media, by Paul Gillin
Jump Start Your Book Sales, Tom and Marilyn Ross
The Portable Writer's Conference: Your Guide to Getting and Staying Published, Stephen Blake Mettee
Speak and Grow Rich, by Dottie Walters and Lilly Walters
Writer's Market, Writer's Digest Books

Index

About the Author

Stephanie Chandler is the author of *From Entrepeneur to Infopreneur: Make Money With Books, E-books and Information Products* and *The Business Startup Checklist and Planning Guide: Seize Your Entrepreneurial Dreams!* She is also the founder of BusinessInfoGuide.com, a directory of resources for entrepreneurs and the owner of Pro Publishing Services, a custom business writing and marketing service that specializes in electronic newsletters.

A frequent speaker at business events and on the radio, Stephanie is a prolific writer whose articles have been seen in dozens of publications. She has also been featured in *Entrepreneur Magazine*, *Business Week*, and the *Los Angeles Times*.

Stephanie resides near Sacramento with her husband, teenage stepson, and her toddler son, a little tornado with a hearty laugh who rocks her world.

Visit her Web sites:

BusinessInfoGuide.com
ProPublishingServices.com
StephanieChandler.com